CU01272118

'I was brought up believing it's a good
would push all Jews into the sea. Ant
whether subconscious bias had left me I
tory tell me no, and such confident yet n
Anthologising this phenomenon is vital work.'

Rachel Riley, *MBE, TV presenter, activist against antisemitism
and advocate for women and girls in STEM*

'Essential and compelling reading on the 7 October attacks by a distinguished
array of historians, lawyers, feminists, novelists and sociologists, who debate
the significance of the Hamas kill-raid against Israel and analyse the denial,
glorification and trivialisation that followed.'

Simon Sebag Montefiore, *historian, author of*
Jerusalem: the biography

'Absolutely and heartbreakingly necessary: some of the greatest thinkers of
our day addressing the worst Jewish trauma in most people's living memory.'

Hadley Freeman, *journalist*

'We were promised "Never Again." As shocking as was the pogrom of
October 7, 2023, no less distressing is how the public square and academy
resonated with the cacophony of sympathizers. These essential volumes of
reflections and analyses will long stand as a landmark in understanding this
contemporary outrage.'

Ilan Troen, *Professor Emeritus of Israel Studies at Brandeis
University and Modern History at Ben-Gurion University,
and Founding Editor of* Israel Studies

'Following the horrifying blow of the atrocities of October 7th came the additional shock that virulent antisemitism had actually intensified in its aftermath. In this upside down moral universe feeling has sometimes overwhelmed
reflection. But this magnificent collection of essays, at once deeply felt and
sharply thought, is an anchorage for the intellect to confront the poisoned
madness of this moment. It ought to be compulsory reading.'

Simon Schama, *historian*

Responses to 7 October: Universities

One of three volumes responding to the 7 October attack, *Universities* focuses on the heartland of contemporary antisemitic thinking, which is scholarship; and its reflection in student discourse on campus.

Contributions go back to Sartre and to debates of Marx's time; another looks at the *New Left* forged in the civil rights movement, and shows how antisemitic responses to the 2023 violence were anticipated by some of the responses to the 1967 *Arab League* aggression. The feminist movement and 'progressives' more generally come under scrutiny, and there is analysis of antisemitism on campus after 7 October, showing how it is tolerated and protected there; including in archaeological attempts to deny that there is an ancient Jewish history in Israel.

This work will appeal to scholars, students and activists with an interest in antisemitism, Jewish studies and the politics of Israel.

Rosa Freedman is Professor of Law at the University of Reading and Research Fellow at the London Centre for the Study of Contemporary Antisemitism, UK.

David Hirsh is the Academic Director and CEO of the London Centre for the Study of Contemporary Antisemitism and a Senior Lecturer in Sociology at Goldsmiths, University of London, UK.

Studies in Contemporary Antisemitism
Series editors

David Hirsh, *Senior Lecturer in Sociology, Goldsmiths, University of London and Academic Director of the London Centre for the Study of Contemporary Antisemitism*

Rosa Freedman, *Professor in the School of Law, University of Reading and Research Fellow at the London Centre for the Study of Contemporary Antisemitism*

Published in conjunction with the London Centre for the Study of Contemporary Antisemitism, *Studies in Contemporary Antisemitism* is a timely, multidisciplinary book series, drawing primarily, but not exclusively, on the social sciences and the humanities. The series encourages academically rigorous and critical publications across several disciplines and that are explicit in understanding and opposing the presence and ascendancy of contemporary antisemitism in both its theoretical and empirical manifestations. The series provides a unique opportunity to offer an intellectual home for a diversity of works that, taken together, crystallize around the study of contemporary antisemitism. The series consists of research monographs, edited collections and short form titles.

Responses to 7 October: Antisemitic Discourse
Edited by Rosa Freedman and David Hirsh, with Odeliya Lanir Zafir

Responses to 7 October: Law and Society
Edited by Rosa Freedman and David Hirsh, with Odeliya Lanir Zafir

Responses to 7 October: Universities
Edited by Rosa Freedman and David Hirsh, with Odeliya Lanir Zafir

For more information about this series, please visit: www.routledge.com/ studies-in-contemporary-antisemitism/book-series/SICA

Responses to 7 October: Universities

Edited by Rosa Freedman and David Hirsh, with Odeliya Lanir Zafir

Routledge
Taylor & Francis Group

LONDON AND NEW YORK

Designed cover image: 'We will not be erased' by Mina Kupfermann (© 2017) Oil on paper.

First published 2024
by Routledge
4 Park Square, Milton Park, Abingdon, Oxon OX14 4RN

and by Routledge
605 Third Avenue, New York, NY 10158

Routledge is an imprint of the Taylor & Francis Group, an informa business

British Library Cataloguing-in-Publication Data
A catalogue record for this book is available from the British Library

ISBN: 978-1-032-80480-4 (hbk)
ISBN: 978-1-032-80556-6 (pbk)
ISBN: 978-1-003-49742-4 (ebk)

DOI: 10.4324/9781003497424

Typeset in Times New Roman
by KnowledgeWorks Global Ltd.

Contents

List of Contributors

Daniel Chernilo is Professor of Sociology at Universidad Adolfo Ibáñez and a Visiting Professor of Social and Political Thought at Loughborough. He has written widely on the history of social thought, humanism, nationalism and cosmopolitanism and is currently working on antisemitism and secularisation. He is a Research Fellow at the London Centre for the Study of Contemporary Antisemitism.

Rebecca Cypess is Professor of Music and faculty affiliate in Jewish Studies at Rutgers University, USA. Her recent publications include *Women and Musical Salons in the Enlightenment* (2022) and the co-edited collection *Music and Jewish Culture in Early Modern Italy* (2022), which received the Solie Award from the American Musicological Society.

Chad Alan Goldberg is Martindale-Bascom Professor of Sociology and an affiliate of the Department of History and Mosse/Weinstein Center for Jewish Studies at the University of Wisconsin-Madison, USA. His books include *Modernity and the Jews in Western Social Thought* (2017). He is a research fellow at the London Centre for the Study of Contemporary Antisemitism.

Eric Heinze is Professor of Law at QMUL (Maitrise *distinction*, Paris; JD *cum laude*, Harvard; Doctoraat *cum laude*, Leiden). His books include *The Most Human Right* (2022), *Hate Speech and Democratic Citizenship* (2016), *The Concept of Injustice* (Routledge, 2012), and *The Logic of Equality* (Routledge, 2005). He has received the following awards: Fulbright-Utrecht, DAAD-Berlin, Chateaubriand-Paris, Nuffield-UK, Harvard-USA, HERA-EU.

Kara Jesella has a BA in Women's Studies, a PhD in Performance Studies, and was the Managing Editor of a feminist academic journal. She is the co-author of the cultural history *How Sassy Changed My Life: A Love Letter to the Greatest Teen Magazine of All Time.*

Günther Jikeli holds the Erna B. Rosenfeld Professorship at the Institute for the Study of Contemporary Antisemitism in the Borns Jewish Studies

Program at Indiana University, USA. He is an Associate Professor in Germanic Studies and Jewish Studies and heads the research lab 'Social Media & Hate.'

Brett Kaufman is an archaeologist, Semitic languages specialist, and Assistant Professor of the Classics at University of Illinois Urbana-Champaign, USA. His research has been funded by the National Science Foundation, the National Geographic Society, the National Natural Science Foundation of China, and the Getty Research Institute.

Susie Linfield is Professor of Journalism at New York University, USA. She is author of *The Cruel Radiance: Photography and Political Violence* and *The Lions' Den: Zionism and the Left from Hannah Arendt to Noam Chomsky.*

Linda Maizels is an independent scholar whose recent book *What is Antisemitism? A Contemporary Introduction* was published by Routledge in September 2022. She earned her PhD from the Hebrew University of Jerusalem with her dissertation *'Charter Members of the Fourth World': Jewish Student Identity and the 'New Antisemitism' on American Campuses, 1967-1994.*

Cary Nelson is Jubilee Professor of Liberal Arts and Sciences Emeritus at the University of Illinois at Urbana-Champaign, USA, and the author or editor of 36 books. His latest is *Hate Speech and Academic Freedom: The Antisemitic Assault on Basic Principles* (2024). He is a Research Fellow at the London Centre for the Study of Contemporary Antisemitism.

Derek Spitz is a commercial and competition law barrister at One Essex Court, UK. He is a Trustee of the London Centre for the Study of Contemporary Antisemitism. He acted for Campaign Against Antisemitism in the EHRC's Investigation into Antisemitism in the Labour Party. He is a co-editor and author of *Constitutional Law of South Africa.*

Introduction

Rosa Freedman and David Hirsh

We, at the *London Centre for the Study of Contemporary Antisemitism* (LCSCA), felt that the events of 7 October 2023 and their aftermath warranted the swift publication of an anthology of short responses by academics and writers. Scholars of antisemitism, law, sociology, human rights, genocide studies, critical theory, politics, linguistics, musicology, psychology and philosophy moved quickly to write in answer to our open call for contributions. Their pieces are urgent, thoughtful, angry, reflective, raw and profound, and diverse.

Many Jews, both in Israel and around the world, and many others too, feel that 7 October constitutes a watershed moment; a moment that separates the before from the after. This anthology across three volumes cannot adequately respond to 7 October. Its meaning, let alone the responses to it, has not yet crystallised. At the same time, for so many of us, there is already a sense that life is divided between before and after.

7 October ought to have been a time when people around the world showed empathy, sympathy and/or solidarity towards Jews and Israel. The scale and nature of those atrocities ought to have shocked the world to its core. Certainly, there is precedent for such sympathy, empathy and/or solidarity for other victims of mass terrorist atrocities.

While many did, other reactions were quite the opposite.

In the hours and days following the massacre, academics, writers, politicians and others, who one might have anticipated would be empathetic with the victims, seemed determined to find reasons to ration their empathy or withdraw it altogether. The tactics used were typical DARVO – deny, attack, and reverse victim and offender. Some of them explicitly welcomed the attack, glorifying it as resistance. Others trivialised it, by immediately weighing the atrocities in a balance against Israeli crimes: real, exaggerated, invented or anticipated. Sometimes all of these responses came from the same individual.

Some people located the shock of 7 October in the fact that, even firmly within the territory of the state of Israel, Jews called for help that day and it did not come, which resonates with a more general Jewish experience of being abandoned to antisemitic violence, throughout history. Many Jews had previously retained some hope that when others saw what could really happen, they would better understand Jewish feelings of precariousness, even in a world with an apparently secure Israel. After 7 October that hope, that if others really saw, they would stand with Jews, was diminished. We were confronted by the opposite, for example, one well-known antizionist was thrilled, exclaiming on X, on the morning of 7 October, 'This is what the liberation will look like.'

It was not only individuals or groups of people who reacted in that way. Institutions, ranging from the global to the local, from the United Nations to generally respected media organisations, from political parties to charities and NGOs, from universities to football clubs. Of course not all of them, although many more stayed silent, but enough to make it clear that Jews cannot count on sympathy, empathy and solidarity, even in the darkest times.

But why does this matter? Why is it significant? And why, for many of us, does this mean that the world and our lives are divided into the before and the after of 7 October?

A core part of antisemitism is the othering of Jews: treating Jews differently to other people or treating the Jewish state differently to other countries. This may take place through law, politics and institutions. It may manifest in practice, by having different expectations or demanding different things of Jews or Israel to other people or other countries, or denying them the same rights as other people or countries. It may also occur through conflating the two, and therefore holding Jews around the world accountable for the actions of Israel or the Israeli government.

Until 7 October many of us thought that the institutions and people with whom we work might be against the Israeli occupation, or even antizionist, but that it did not necessarily make them antisemitic. Since 7 October this confidence, this willingness to give the benefit of the doubt, has been diminished. For some, it underscored their belief that there would never be a time when the left would stand with Jews, stand up for Jews, or treat Jews as though they count. For others, this was the dawn of that realisation.

When we put out a call for contributions, for short perspectives, for responses to 7 October, we did not imagine the dozens of drafts that would land on our desks within weeks. We did not realise the strength of feeling from our colleagues, friends and strangers around the world. So much so that we have created a three-volume anthology to house and showcase that work, and even then we did not have room for all of the submissions we received. The three volumes reflect the three main themes of those contributions: law and society; universities; and antisemitic discourse. While each provides a standalone contribution, the anthology is designed to be read as a whole, and there are cross-cutting themes throughout.

Editor's Note

To date, there is no final number of those killed in the 7 October massacre. As of 14 January 2024, over 1,200 victims of the terror attack have been publicly identified, including 790 civilians and among them 65 foreign citizens.[1] A further 314 Israeli soldiers[2] and 60 police officers[3] were killed on the day of the massacre. Some 136 people injured on October 7 later died in hospitals from their wounds.[4] The remains of 24 people are being held hostage by Hamas in Gaza, some killed by Hamas in captivity and others during the initial assault.[5]

Throughout the volume when discussing the victims of 7 October, the figure of 1,200 will be reflected as the most reliable count available to us. With the situation still unfolding, the number may change further by the time this anthology is released.

Notes

1 'Swords of Iron: War in the South - Hamas' Attack on Israel'. (2023). *Ministry of Foreign Affairs of Israel* [Press Release]. Available at: https://www.gov.il/en/departments/news/swords-of-iron-war-in-the-south-7-oct-2023 (Accessed: 15 January 2024). See the full list of names of civilian victims at: https://www.gov.il/en/departments/news/swords-of-iron-civilian-casualties#Civilian%20casualties

2 'Swords of Iron: Israel Police, Security Forces (Shabak) and First Responders Casualties'. (2023). *Ministry of Foreign Affairs of Israel* [Press Release]. Available at: https://www.gov.il/en/departments/news/swords-of-iron-israel-police-security-forces-casualties (Accessed: 15 January 2024).

3 'Swords of Iron: IDF Casualties'. (2023). *Ministry of Foreign Affairs of Israel* [Press Release]. Available at: https://www.gov.il/en/Departments/news/swords-of-iron-idf-casualties (Accessed: 15 January 2024).

4 Swords of Iron: War in the South - Hamas' Attack on Israel'. (2023). *Ministry of Foreign Affairs of Israel* [Press Release]. Available at: https://www.gov.il/en/departments/news/swords-of-iron-war-in-the-south-7-oct-2023 (Accessed: 15 January 2024).

5 Ibid.

1 'A Tool to Advance Imperial Interests'

Leftist Self-Scrutiny and Israeli Wrongdoing

Eric Heinze[1]

Writing shortly after the assault of 7 October 2023 in which Hamas killed or took hostage more than 1,400 Israelis, Mikael Wolfe, a Stanford University historian, wrote, 'Denying the *history* of settler-colonialism only perpetuates suffering in Israel and Palestine.'[2] Also writing after the invasion was Wesam Ahmad, a Palestinian human rights advocate who charged that 'international justice, more often than not, is used as a tool to advance imperial interests, and not justice.' In Ahmad's view, this has long been 'known by anyone who has ever examined, even superficially, the *history* of imperialism, from the European scramble for Africa to more recent United States interventions in Latin America.'[3]

I do not know whether or in what sense Wolfe or Ahmad might call themselves 'leftist'. After all, terms like 'left' or 'progressive' can mean many things. Yet these and numerous other arguments have guided leftist attitudes toward Israel.[4] According to these arguments, we in the West must learn our history as an exercise in collective self-scrutiny. We must bury old tales that the West has played a civilising role in the world. We must understand Western oppression long waged against disempowered populations for the benefit of white elites. Call it a 'leftist' reading of history, yet it has also influenced strands of mainstream opinion that place the blame for Palestinian suffering on Israel. Many on the left believe that we can credibly speak about Israel-Palestine only when we have publicly and vigorously engaged with these histories. (I shall use the phrase 'public and vigorous' throughout this chapter to distinguish broad-based engagement from the more rarefied discussions that might emerge in textbooks or seminar rooms.)

I certainly sympathise with any position which states that history must teach self-critical analysis instead of myth-making. Yet if leftists are exhorting us to plunge into critical histories of the West, then what do they think about the left's own historical allegiances to brutal regimes dating back over more than a century? If leftists are teaching our history to us, then who is teaching their history to them? In response to these questions, leftists commonly cite their traditions of collective self-scrutiny, sometimes known as *autocritique*, whereby they

DOI: 10.4324/9781003497424-1

revise their ideas as circumstances change.[5] For example, many may have supported Joseph Stalin, Mao Zedong, Kim Il Sung, or Pol Pot but they have since learned their lessons. So a kind of bargain is at work: given that leftists re-evaluate their own histories, they can justifiably demand that the rest of us publicly and vigorously engage with Western wrongdoings, including Israeli policy and perhaps even Israel's very creation.

But have leftists held up their end of the bargain? As we will see, leftists' self-scrutiny has been an illusion. They have engaged in it only when their political agendas stood to gain and, on their own criteria, self-scrutiny hampered by political self-interest is not self-scrutiny at all. Following their own precepts, leftists cannot credibly speak about Israel-Palestine until they have *publicly and vigorously* engaged in a critical history of leftist wrongdoing, which must include histories of antisemitism waged by regimes and movements that have been widely supported on the left.

The Radical Critique of Western Liberal Democracy

So yes, words like 'left' and 'progressive' can indeed mean many things yet these terms have not been so open-ended as to lack all meaning. A roomful of leftists may disagree about which candidates to support, or how to set tax rates, or how to prioritise government spending. Yet they overwhelmingly agree on one precept, which I shall call The Radical Critique of Western Liberal Democracy. It can be summarised as follows: *Over several centuries, Western societies have damaged millions of lives through militarism, economic exploitation, colonialism, racism, patriarchy, heteronormativity, and other forms of injustice on a global scale. Yes, such evils have also arisen outside Western societies, yet their Western versions have proved to be extensive, systemic (or 'structural'), and exceptionally destructive.*[6]

Of course, any visitor to cities like Beijing or Mumbai will know that nowadays no clear lines separate 'Western' from 'non-Western'.[7] Yet what is crucial about the Radical Critique is that Western liberal democracies do not expressly justify their laws and policies on the kinds of grounds that would have been familiar several centuries ago, such as royal descent or military conquest. Above all, we recite universal values of what are sometimes referred to as 'classically liberal' norms such as civic equality, economic opportunity, human dignity, individual autonomy, and even-handed application of the rule of law. When Karl Marx blasted these norms, it was not because he disliked them but because they promised a world precisely opposite to the one he saw around him. Lawmakers and courts were invoking these norms to entrench brutal hierarchies, so these norms lacked all meaning for ordinary workers whilst all benefits accrued to property-owning elites.[8]

What is equally paramount for the Radical Critique are the ways in which history is presented to the public. For the left it cannot suffice that critical histories end up tucked away in textbooks and lecture halls. If ideas are to spur change then they must spread to homes, workplaces, and onto the streets. Classism, racism, colonialism, or patriarchy never arose solely from isolated acts of violence and discrimination but always had deeper roots in public consciousness.[9] In the same way, the West's self-scrutiny must begin in primary schools[10] and continue into higher education,[11] also taking place in the private sector[12] and through film, television, radio, music, and social media.[13]

This view of history has guided the following attitude toward Israel. First, Western colonial and neo-colonial power has been founded on racist assumptions of white supremacy prevailing over the supposed backwardness of non-Western peoples, with Israeli statehood forming part of that story.[14] Second, like other Western nations, Israel justifies its existence by reciting classically liberal values of equality, opportunity, dignity, autonomy, and the rule of law,[15] yet in practice these norms have been applied to entrench Jewish privilege, creating anti-Palestinian apartheid.[16] Third, none of us can meaningfully speak about Israel and Palestine until we have publicly and vigorously engaged with this longer history of Western oppression.[17]

Autocritique and Interest-Convergence

At this point a typical move for defenders of Israel would be to respond by dissecting these three theses step by step. Some might insist that Israel's founding cannot be equated with 19th century settler colonialism or with the kinds of 20th and 21st century neo-colonial policies that are attributed to other Western powers. Others might claim that Israel, although no more innocent of racism than countless other nations, cannot be called racist in any exceptional sense and is indeed less racist than many of the nations that censure it. And then others might argue that Israel, far from one-sidedly committing racist discrimination, must navigate an environment in which antisemitism too counts among the racisms that have fuelled hostilities in the Middle East and indeed across the globe.

Since other writers have already penned these rebuttals, my focus will be different. I will not challenge the Radical Critique on its own terms. In fact, I believe it holds valuable ideas. Instead, my question will be: What follows if we accept the premise that critical histories of the West must be disseminated to reach the widest possible public? What does this mean for the left's own histories? To answer these questions, and to explain why they matter, let me first take a detour.

In 1980 Harvard Professor Derrick Bell published what later became a foundational article. Bell proposed a theory of 'interest-convergence', explaining that throughout US history the white establishment had granted rights to ethnic minorities only when doing so promoted white interests.[18] As an aside, I should note that we could poke holes around the edges of this theory. After all, throughout the ages political power has always relied upon interest-convergence. This never applied more to whites than to other elites in history. Wherever we find powerful factions, we rarely find them acting against their perceived interests – even when those perceptions turn out to be misguided, as they certainly were among whites who feared black equality. Yet ultimately this qualification serves to strengthen Bell's thesis not to weaken it. It applies to white power precisely because it has always applied to political power.

Rather, the real problem I see is a different one: very little energy has been devoted to examining interest-convergence on the left itself. Have leftists pursued their own norms of public and vigorous self-scrutiny irrespective of perceived gains or losses for their political goals? Let's run through a few examples. Some 20th and 21st century writers have sought to rethink Marxism in ways that would avoid totalitarianism, dating back to intellectuals such as Max Horkheimer, Theodor Adorno, or Louis Althusser – and more recently, including authors such as Alain Badiou, Wendy Brown, Judith Butler, Cornel West, or Slavoj Žižek. Yet in the years these more recent authors were writing, the left's Stalinist and Maoist pasts had long become a liability. Despite some assorted strays who might still admire Stalin or Mao, a strategy of self-scrutiny served to distance the left from those horrendous pasts, which conspicuously served leftist interests.

Or consider some other voices on the left, for example, within feminism or LGBTQ+ politics. By the final decades of the 20th century, women from ethnic minority and non-Western backgrounds increasingly accused the left of harboring white, middle-class biases. Progressive feminists like to highlight their collective self-scrutiny because they took these reproaches on board, opening the doors to ethnic minority, non-Western, and other perspectives.[19] That same shift occurred in LGBTQ+ politics, which, too, had been inaugurated in the West largely by middle-class whites but then broadened to include a greater range of voices.[20]

At first glance, leftists might well have seemed to be practicing self-scrutiny in these situations, yet these ethnic minority and third-world voices had long ago adopted the Radical Critique. In all three examples – post-Marxist politics, feminist politics, and LGBTQ+ politics – the criticisms that progressives embraced, far from seriously challenging the Radical Critique, were massively reinforcing it. Interest-convergence in these three settings was so conspicuous that it becomes doubtful whether leftists were seriously practicing self-scrutiny at all. To be fair, leftists are no worse at self-scrutiny than anyone else. Conservatives – the clue is in the name – can hardly be called pioneers of critical reflection about historical injustices. Yet it is leftists themselves who have set their own bar higher by promising an autocritique that they have never delivered, at least not outside the cloistered walls of their seminar rooms and meeting halls.

Autocritique and Antisemitism

How have these failures of self-scrutiny marred leftists' attitudes toward Jews? Plenty of histories probe antisemitism amid figures on or influential within the left dating back to the 19th century, including figures such as Mikhail Bakunin, Pierre-Joseph Proudhon, Keir Hardie, Sidney Webb, or Ernest Bevin.[21] Yet for Israel-Palestine today, the immediately relevant histories arise from the left's – admittedly variable, yet often considerable – support for socialist dictatorships[22] that were engaged in all and sundry anti-Jewish policies, both overt and covert. These too have been extensively researched so for now I shall recall only some highlights.

For example, during the Cold War, Kremlin authorities never officially denied the Holocaust and facts about raw numbers of deaths were not suppressed. Rather, what was crushed was any discussion of it *as* anti-Jewish persecution, or indeed any open examination of historical antisemitism, which would have spurred questions about anti-Jewish purges taking place in the Soviet Union itself and in various satellite states in ways that were never rigorously challenged on the Western left aside from a few scattered voices. Instead, Moscow's tactic was to lump antisemitism together with all other forms of racism and discrimination, which were packaged as essentially right-wing, having been effectively overcome under socialism.[23] The Kremlin manoeuvre was to present racism and imperialism as Western evils, all part of 'the highest form of capitalism.'[24] Suddenly it was simply Russian, simply Ukrainian, simply Belarusian, simply Polish, simply Czech, simply Lithuanian, simply Hungarian, simply Romanian, and other civilians defined solely in national terms, whom Nazis had deported and exterminated, with no reference to their Jewish identities, despite the proportions of Jews from those places having been vastly greater.[25]

In a word, the Holocaust was never solely a Nazi story. Yet in the Soviet sphere, World War Two was taught only via sanitised narratives about Soviet heroism, rarely with concerted objections from the Western left. As is customary for state propaganda, these were not outright lies yet suppressed elements of the Holocaust that raised questions about Moscow's own tactical antisemitism. Well into the 1980s, while important tranches of the left still supported the Soviet Union, Central and Eastern Europe lacked anything like what in the West had come to be known as Holocaust Education. That very phrase found no currency in official discourses within the Soviet sphere during the Cold War, nor was it easy to identify leftists willing to condemn this whitewashing. Meanwhile, periodic purges had proceeded in vintage Soviet fashion, with Jews often disparaged not *as* Jews, in the manner of the far right, but as 'bourgeois capitalists,' 'enemies of the workers,' and the like. Unsurprisingly, in post-Soviet Central and Eastern Europe today, nationalists have handily re-packaged antisemitism via coded references to 'liberals,' 'foreign agents,' and 'capitalists.'[26]

Admittedly, few Western leftists expressly condoned, for example, antisemitic campaigns in the Soviet Union, Poland, or East Germany during the Cold War, as there was no gain for the left in doing so. Yet nor were those campaigns ever a deal-breaker among those leftists who would have seen little gain in condemning Soviet antisemitism because it would have jeopardised their own historical profile. In a nutshell, leftists have willingly condemned antisemitism but only in two ways. First, they expressly condemn it wherever they can broadly identify or define it as right-wing, yet there is patent interest-convergence in chastising the right since any such stance reinforces the left-ism of leftist politics. Second, when leftists do condemn incidents of left-wing antisemitism, it is only by packaging them as errors and aberrations, never as systemic (or 'structural') on the left.[27]

From a leftist standpoint, whites act unjustly when they deny responsibil-ity for racist or colonial practices that took place before they were born. This is why leftists correctly insist on public and vigorous scrutiny of Western op-pression. So it would be inadmissible for leftists to deny responsibility for decades-long leftist support for regimes that existed before they were born. Leftists must start to exhibit the same public and vigorous scrutiny of their own past commitments to regimes that brutalised innocent lives to the tune of tens of millions,[28] with Jews too figuring on that list.

Autocritique and Israel

Leftists have failed, then, to undertake public and vigorous scrutiny of the left's own historical commitments to murderous regimes (again, regardless of whether these topics were occasionally broached in textbooks or classrooms). What are the consequences for attitudes toward Israel? Here too, the chron-icle is long so for now I shall cite only one example. After defecting from Ceauşescu's Romania in the 1970s, the senior intelligence officer Ion Pacepa documented how the Soviet secret police had identified Muslims' anti-Israel animus as a golden opportunity. Viewing Muslims as ignorant and impres-sionable, the Kremlin's Secret Police chief and later Secretary General Yuri Andropov undertook a program of sowing antisemitic propaganda throughout Muslim populations. In Andropov's view, 'We needed to instil a Nazi-style hatred for the Jews throughout the Islamic world, and to turn this weapon of the emotions into a terrorist bloodbath against Israel.'[29] Suddenly the *Protocols of the Elders of Zion* were displayed for sale in Muslim countries as far away as Malaysia, with passages translated verbatim into the 1988 Hamas Charter.[30]

Despite the attention that the left has long devoted to the Israel-Palestine conflict[31] as reproducing Western orientalism,[32] progressives have spent lit-tle time examining the Kremlin's orientalist campaigns aimed at exploiting a stupid and violent Islamic world. The Soviets spread Jew hatred across Mus-lim nations with few objections from Western leftists. To this day the *Proto-cols* circulate in Muslim countries with few questions asked on the left about whether they bear responsibility for this history in the way the rest of us must be held to account for Western orientalism. Those who rightly exhort us to learn about orientalism in the West have shown little interest in teaching about how that same poison infused their own political allegiances. Needless to say, highlighting one form of discrimination does not mean denying another, and the globalisation of Soviet-spawned antisemitism by no means implies that racism has been one-sided. Clearly, anti-Muslim racisms from the West[33] have further fuelled Israel-Palestine enmities. Nevertheless, lacking any interest-convergence, the left never launched campaigns to teach public and vigorous histories of leftist antisemitism, though any serious autocritique would have meant that they should have been actively disseminating such knowledge directly alongside programs to teach critical histories of the West.

Throughout public and private sectors, including primary, secondary, and higher education, training programs have become routine to teach us about historical exclusion lurking behind the West's professed values of dignity, equality, and opportunity, as witnessed in events such as Black History Days, Women's History Days, or LGBTQ+ History Days. Yet imagine for a moment something like a 'Socialist History Day', which would take a similarly critical look at forms of historical exclusion, including antisemitism, lurking behind the left's professed values of political liberation, social equality, and other such ideals, showing how dictatorships enjoying substantial leftist support invoked leftist norms to enforce the diametrically opposed realities of hierarchy and privilege for elites at the expense of exclusion and disempowerment for millions of ordinary people.

Nowhere have leftists undertaken any such events or training programs. In fact, notice that the very idea of a critically structured 'Socialist History Day' sounds bizarre because we have so deeply assimilated the assumption that the only histories to be publicly and vigorously scrutinised are those of major Western powers. Nevertheless, following the left's own logic honed for more than a century, *leftists cannot claim to speak credibly on Israel-Palestine without first engaging in public and vigorous scrutiny of mass injustices, including campaigns of antisemitism, long committed by regimes supported on the left.*

Imagine an alternative left, which would have engaged in public self-scrutiny such that a 'Socialist History Day,' instead of sounding odd, would sound routine to our ears. Imagine this environment in which, over decades, the left would have pushed for public education about leftist support for heinous regimes on a par with education about Western wrongdoings. In that environment, some attitudes toward Israel might have turned out rather different. Leftists such as Badiou,[34] Brown,[35] Butler,[36] West,[37] and Žižek[38] have gleefully condemned right-wing antisemitism because the leftist interest-convergence was manifest. Yet while they might breezily acknowledge incidents of specifically leftist antisemitism, none of them have ever launched any public and vigorous autocritique regarding those histories.

Can I prove that these writers would have nuanced their views about Israel-Palestine had they grown up within that more seriously self-critical leftist milieu? Sadly, history never discloses its alternatives so I can prove no such thing. These writers might have participated in initiatives like a pervasively self-critical Socialist History Day while still publishing the views they in fact ended up taking. Yet then a new puzzle would have emerged:

Why would leftist critiques of the West so massively inflect their discussions about Israel whilst leftist critiques of the left would have no such impact?

Of course, some observers might freely concede the histories of leftist support for nominally socialist dictatorships while insisting that progressives' tasks have never been to critique injustice generally but only to focus on Western liberal democracies. Yet the problem is that such a stance would dismantle any pretence that the left had ever valued autocritique where interest-convergence was lacking. It would mean that the left had only ever acted tribally, zealously advocating for victims of its rivals' politics while sidestepping equal or greater numbers of victims of its own politics. Alternatively, consider the following claim: 'Most progressives have already conceded that the left wrongly supported brutal regimes, and leftists have condemned any antisemitism in which those regimes were active or complicit. So it is wrong to argue that the left needs such public and vigorous engagement with its history.' Yet as soon as we transpose that claim to the Radical Critique, it collapses. For example, imagine a leftist student group applying for permission to hold a Black History Day or a Colonial History Day, and then university authorities issuing the following reply: 'Our nation has already acknowledged that Western governments wrongly supported brutal policies and we condemn all forms of racism. So there are no grounds for insisting that the West needs such public and vigorous engagement with its history.' Far from sounding reasoned or measured, such a response would itself appear to many leftists as racist.

*

To conclude, core claims made over decades by progressives have presupposed that we must publicly disseminate collective self-scrutiny about Western histories of racism and colonialism. Yet despite much lip-service paid to autocritique, leftists have never engaged in collective self-scrutiny without some prospect of political gain, so on their own terms they have never really engaged in it at all. They have inscribed Israel-Palestine within critical histories of Western racism and colonialism, whilst exempting their own political homes from any public and vigorous scrutiny of the left's own support for regimes massively implicated in histories of antisemitism. On their own criteria, it remains doubtful whether leftists can claim credibility until they have initiated campaigns of public and vigorous critique of antisemitism committed by regimes that have long enjoyed support from the Western left.

Notes

1 © Eric Heinze, 2024. The author thanks Rosa Freedman, David Hirsh, and Odeliya Lanir Zafir for the interest they have taken in this chapter. All references to online resources are verified as of 2 Jan. 2023.
2 Wolfe, M. 'Denying the history of settler-colonialism only perpetuates suffering in Israel and Palestine', *The Stanford Daily*, 31 Oct. 2023, https://stanforddaily.com/2023/10/31/from-the-community-denying-the-history-of-settler-colonialism-only-perpetuates-suffering-in-israel-and-palestine/ (emphasis added).

3 Ahmad, W. 'The mask is off: Gaza has exposed the hypocrisy of international law', *Al Jazeera*, 17 Oct. 2023, https://www.aljazeera.com/opinions/2023/10/17/the-mask-is-off-gaza-has-exposed-the-hypocrisy-of-international-law (emphasis added).

4 For example, Butler, J. (2012) *Parting Ways: Jewishness and the Critique of Zionism*. New York: Columbia University Press; Chomsky, N. (2016 [1983]) *Fateful Triangle: The United States, Israel, and the Palestinians*, 3rd ed. London: Pluto; Chomsky, N. and Pappé, I. (2015) *On Palestine*. London: Penguin.

5 For example, Morin, E. (1994 [1959]) *Autocritique*. Paris: Seuil; Ignatow, A. (1996) *Zwischen 'Selbstkritik' und neuer Hoffnung: die marxistische Theorie-Debatte in Rußland*. Cologne: Bundesinstitut für ostwissenschaftliche und internationale Studien.

6 The literature is enormous, but typical samples would include Césaire, A. (2000 [1955]) *Discours sur le colonialisme*. Paris: Réclame; Fanon, F. (2004 [1961]) *Les damnés de la terre*. Paris: La Découverte; Fanon, F. (2015 [1952]) *Peau noire, masques blancs*. Paris: Seuil; Nkrumah, K. (1965) *Neo-Colonialism: The Last Stage of Imperialism*. New York: International Publishers; Memmi, A. (2002) *Portrait du colonisé/Portrait du colonisateur*. Paris: Gallimard; Crenshaw, K. W. 'Race, Reform, and Retrenchment: Transformation and Legitimation in Antidiscrimination Law', *Harvard Law Review* 101 (7) (1988) pp. 1331–1387; Mehta, U. S. (1999) *Liberalism and Empire*, 2nd ed. Chicago: University of Chicago Press.

7 Moreover, in some countries, such as Russia or Iran, it is conservatives who voice at least some of these ideas insofar as they fundamentally blame the West for their societies' social ills. See, e.g., Papkova, I. (2011) *The Orthodox Church and Russian Politics*. New York: Oxford University Press; Ghanoonparvar, M. 'Through Tinted Lenses: Iranian and Western Perceptions and Reconstructions of the Other.' In Mahmoud, ed. (2014) *Re-Imagining the Other*. New York: Palgrave-Macmillan, pp. 57–73.

8 For example, Marx, K. (1956+ [1844]) *Zur Judenfrage*, in *Marx—Engels Werke*, 6th ed., vol. 1, Institut für Marxismus-Leninismus, eds. Berlin: Dietz, pp. 347–377; Marx, K. (1956+ [1875]) *Kritik des Gothaer Programms*, in *Marx—Engels Werke*, vol. 19, Institut für Marxismus-Leninismus, eds. Berlin: Dietz, pp. 11–34.

9 See note 5.

10 Examples can be found throughout Western nations, such as *1619 Project,* at *Pulitzer Center* (n.d.), https://pulitzercenter.org/lesson-plan-grouping/1619-project-curriculum; 'Cultivating diversity, equity, and inclusion in education environments', *Resilient Educator,* n.d., https://resilienteducator.com/collections/cultivating-diversity-inclusion-equity/; *Diversity and Inclusion in Schools.* London: Pearson, 2020. https://www.pearson.com/content/dam/one-dot-com/one-dot-com/uk/documents/educator/schools/issues/inclusion/diversity-and-inclusion-in-schools-report.pdf; 'Semaine d'éducation et d'actions contre le racisme et l'antisémitisme', *Ministère de l'Education Nationale et de la Jeunesse*, n.d., https://www.education.gouv.fr/la-semaine-d-education-et-d-actions-contre-le-racisme-et-l-antisemitisme-5204.

11 Examples can be found throughout Western nations, such as 'Creating a more equitable SUNY', *State University of New York (SUNY)*, n.d., https://www.suny.edu/diversity/; 'Delegacion del Rector para la Igualdad', *Universidad Complutense Madrid*, n.d., https://www.ucm.es/unidaddeigualdad/; 'Diversiteit en inclusie', *Universiteit Leiden*, n.d., https://www.universiteitleiden.nl/dossiers/diversiteit; 'Diversity', *University of California*, n.d., https://diversity.universityofcalifornia.edu/index.html; 'Diversity an der Freien Universität Berlin [FUB]', n.d., https://www.fu-berlin.de/sites/diversity/index.html.

12 Examples can be found from many companies, such as 'Creating a culture of diversity, equity and inclusion', *Coca-Cola Company*, n.d., https://www.coca-colacompany.com/social/diversity-and-inclusion; 'Mit Vielfalt die Zukunft gestalten', *Lufthansa Group*, n.d., https://www.lufthansagroup.com/de/verantwortung/soziale-verantwortung/vielfalt-und-chancengleichheit.html.

13 For example, 'Diversity & inclusion', *BBC*, n.d., https://www.bbc.co.uk/diversity/; 'Our commitment to diversity', *NPR*, n.d., https://www.npr.org/diversity; Duncombe, S. and Lambert, S. (2021) *The Art of Activism*. New York: OR Books.

14 See note 9.

15 See Basic Law: Human Dignity and Liberty, adopted by the Knesset on 17 March 1992.

16 For example, Pappé, I. ed. (2015) *Israel and South Africa: The Many Faces of Apartheid*. London: Zed.

17 See notes 2.

18 Bell, D. 'Brown v. Board of Education and the Interest-Convergence Dilemma', *Harvard Law Review* 93 (1980) pp. 518–533.

19 See, e.g., Mohanty, C. T., Russo, A. and Torres, L. eds. (1991) *Third World Women and the Politics of Feminism*. Bloomington: Indiana University Press.

20 See, e.g., Mason, C. L. ed. (2018) *Routledge Handbook of Queer Development Studies*. London: Routledge.

21 Fine, R. and Spencer, P. (2017) *Antisemitism and the Left*. Manchester: Manchester University Press; Dreyfus, M. (2009) *L'antisémitisme à gauche*. Paris: La Découverte; Hanloser, G. ed. (2020) *Linker Antisemitismus?* Vienna: Mandelbaum Verlag; Rich, D. (2016) *The Left's Jewish Problem*. London: Biteback Publishing.

22 On shifting alignments of Western leftist currents with Soviet and Maoist policies, see, e.g., Furet, F. (1995) *Le passé d'une illusion*. Paris: Robert Laffont/Calmann-Lévy; Julliard, J. (2013) *Les Gauches françaises 1762–2012*. Paris: Flammarion, pp. 703–766; Smith, E. and Worley, M. eds. (2014) *Against the Grain: The British Far Left from 1956*. Manchester: Manchester University Press; Smith, E. and Worley, M. eds. (2017) *Waiting for the Revolution: The British Far Left from 1956*. Manchester: Manchester University Press; Thorpe, A. (2015) *A History of the Labour Party*, 4th ed. London: Palgrave.

23 For example, Huttenbach, H. R. ed. (1990) 'Introduction' in Henry R. Huttenbach, *Soviet Nationality Policies: Ruling Ethnic Groups in the USSR*. London: Cassell, pp. 1– 8. Some of the discussion in this section draws from Heinze, E. 'Russia is the global leader in Jew-hate', *Jewish Chronicle*, 24 Feb. 2017, https://www.thejc.com/lets-talk/russia-is-the-global-leader-in-jew-hate-rj66tc71.

24 Cf. Lenin, V. (2010 [1917]) *Imperialism: The Highest Form of Capitalism*, London: Penguin.

25 For example, Küchler, S. 'DDR-Geschichtsbilder', *Internationale Schulbuchforschung* 22 (2000) pp. 31–48; Poltorak, D. and Leshchiner, V. "Teaching the Holocaust in Russia," *Internationale Schulbuchforschung* 22 (2000) pp. 127–134.

26 For example, Azadovskii, K. and Egorov, B. 'From Anti-Westernism to Anti-Semitism', *Journal of Cold War Studies* 4 (2002) pp. 66–80; Jenne, E. K., Bozóki, A. and Visnovitz, P. '2 Antisemitic Tropes, Fifth-Columnism, and "Soros-Bashing".' In Mylonas, H. and Radnitz, S. eds. (2022) *Enemies Within*. Oxford: Oxford University Press, pp. 45–72.

27 For example, Badiou, A. and Winter, C. 'La gifle de Badiou à la rhétorique de Bensussan', *Libération,* 11 Aug. 2014, https://www.liberation.fr/societe/2014/08/11/la-gifle-de-badiou-a-la-rhetorique-de-bensussan_1079119 (retrieved 1 Sept. 2023).

28 See Heinze, E. 'Critical Theory and Memory Politics: Leftist Autocritique After the Ukraine War', *International Journal of Law in Context*, (2023), pp. 1–20. Open-access online: doi:10.1017/S1744552323000289.

29 Pacepa, I. 'Russian footprints', *National Review*, 24 Aug. 2006, https://www.nationalreview.com/2006/08/russian-footprints-ion-mihai-pacepa/.

30 For example, Ben-Itto, H. (2020) *The Lie That Will Not Die*, 2nd ed. London: Vallentine Mitchell; Hagemeister, M. (2021) *The Perennial Conspiracy Theory*. London: Routledge; Cohen, E. B. and Boyd, E. 'The KGB and Anti-Israel Propaganda Operations', *Informing Science* 22 (2019), pp. 157–182.

31 For example, Muhannad, A. M. 'The Jerusalem declaration', *Al Jazeera*, Apr 21, 2021, https://www.aljazeera.com/opinions/2021/4/21/the-jerusalem-declaration-on-antisemitism-is-an-orientalist-text; Ashcroft, B. 'Representation and its discontents', *Religion* 34 (2004), pp. 113–121.

32 For example, Said, E. W. (2003 [1978]) *Orientalism*. London: Penguin.

33 For example, Beydoun, K. A. (2018) *American Islamophobia*. Oakland: University of California.

34 See, e.g., Badiou, A. (2015 [2005]) *Portées du Mot "juif"*. Paris: Léo Scheer; Alain and Winter, note 27.

35 See, e.g., Brown, W. 'Rights and Identity in Late Modernity.' In Sarat, A. and Kearns, T. R. eds. (1995) *Identities, Politics, and Rights*. Ann Arbor: University of Michigan, pp. 85–130.

36 See Butler, note 4.

37 See, e.g., Samuels, B. 'Cornel West', *Haaretz*, 14 Mar. 2021, https://www.haaretz.com/us-news/2021-03-14/ty-article/.highlight/cornel-west-explains-why-hes-convinced-his-views-on-israel-led-him-out-of-harvard/0000017f-f51d-dddc-abff-fd7d9d880000.

38 See, e.g., Žižek, S. 'There is no conflict', *Independent*, 5 Dec. 2019 (amending version of 3 Dec. 2019), https://www.independent.co.uk/voices/labour-jeremy-corbyn-antisemitism-zionism-israel-slavoj-zizek-a9231006.html.

2 Murder and Moral Responsibility

Thinking with and against Sartre about Reactions to the October 7th Pogrom

Chad Alan Goldberg

When I committed to teaching a new course on the history of antisemitism in the Fall 2023 semester at the large, Midwestern, public university where I work, I expected the course to be timely. I knew that antisemitism has increased since the beginning of the twenty-first century and spikes during violence in the Israeli-Palestinian conflict and wars in the Middle East. But I had no idea just how timely the course would become about one month into the new semester.

On October 7, 2023, as thousands of rockets launched from Gaza fell on Israeli homes and a hospital in the city of Ashkelon, an estimated 3,000 terrorists invaded multiple towns and communities in southern Israel, massacred some 1,200 people, wounded or injured several times that number, and abducted some 240 people to hold as hostages in Gaza.[1] The perpetrators were armed members of Hamas, an acronym for Islamic Resistance Movement, an organization designated as a terrorist organization by numerous countries and international entities, including the United States, Canada, the Organization of American States, the European Union, the United Kingdom, Australia, New Zealand, and Japan.[2] Its founding charter cites *The Protocols of the Elders of Zion* as an authoritative source and calls for the genocide of the Jewish people.[3] The vast majority of the victims of the October 7th terrorist attacks were civilians; they included the elderly, Holocaust survivors, women, babies, children, young families, and young people attending a music festival, as well as US and other foreign nationals. They were slaughtered, mutilated, raped, and burned. According to a statement signed on October 15, 2023, by more than 100 experts on international law, these atrocities constitute war crimes, violations of international law, and, insofar as they 'appear to have been carried out with an "intent to destroy, in whole or in part" a national group—Israelis—a goal explicitly declared by Hamas, they most probably constitute an international crime of genocide.'[4] As if to confirm this assessment, senior Hamas official Ghazi Hamad declared in early November 2023 that Hamas intends to repeat the October 7th atrocities until Israel is annihilated. 'On October 7, October 10, October one-millionth,' Hamad declared, 'everything we do is justified.'[5]

DOI: 10.4324/9781003497424-2

One might expect such barbarism to shock the conscience of the world and elicit swift and vigorous condemnation. After all, condemnation of such atrocities does not entail the endorsement of Israel's decades-long military occupation of the territories it captured in the 1967 Six Day War or the far-right government that has led Israel since December 2022, both of which many Israelis oppose. And, indeed, swift, strong, and unequivocal condemnations came from US President Joe Biden and European Union President Ursula von der Leyen, among others.[6] But we have also witnessed another kind of reaction, very different and deeply disturbing. Some on the political left have not merely expressed support for the Palestinian cause but, in some cases, have praised and defended the October 7th pogrom. Such reactions came notably in the United States from local chapters of Black Lives Matter and Democratic Socialists of America. 'When a people have been subject to decades of apartheid and unimaginable violence, their resistance must not be condemned, but understood as a desperate act of self-defense,' Black Lives Matter Los Angeles declared on social media on October 9.[7] New York City's chapter of Democratic Socialists of America held a celebratory rally on the day after the October 7th pogrom, prompting some progressive members of the US Congress with ties to the organization to criticize or distance themselves from it.[8] The chapter responded to criticism by apologizing for the timing of the rally, but it refused to condemn Hamas for the atrocities it committed.[9]

Praise for and defense of the October 7th pogrom is not limited to what the Anti-Defamation League calls 'fringe-left groups'; it has also been visible at major universities in Europe and the United States.[10] This reaction should not be dismissed, then, as merely an expression of emotional outrage; rather, we are witnessing educated elites elaborating intellectual justifications for violence against Jews. Faculty members, teaching fellows, researchers, and doctoral candidates affiliated with elite institutions like Columbia University, the London School of Economics, and the University of California immediately praised the October 7th pogrom for demonstrating that decolonization is not 'just a theory' or a 'metaphor.'[11] Erwin Chemerinsky, the dean of the University of California Berkeley School of Law, noted similar reactions: 'A Columbia professor [Joseph Massad, on October 8] called the Hamas massacre "awesome" and a "stunning victory." A Yale professor [Zareena Grewal] tweeted [on October 7], "It's been such an extraordinary day!" while calling Israel a "murderous, genocidal settler state." A Chicago art professor [Mika Tosca] posted a note [on October 17] reading, "Israelis are pigs. Savages. Very very bad people. Irredeemable excrement …. May they all rot in hell." A UC Davis professor [Jemma Decristo] tweeted [on October 10], "Zionist journalists … have houses w[ith] addresses, kids in school," adding "they can fear their bosses, but they should fear us more."'[12]

Praise for and defense of the October 7th pogrom has come from university students as well as their teachers. A statement written by the Harvard Undergraduate Palestine Solidarity Committee and co-signed by 33 other Harvard student organizations on October 7 held 'the Israeli regime entirely responsible for all unfolding violence.'[13] Students for Justice in Palestine has expressed open support for the October 7th pogrom. National Students for Justice in Palestine called the terror attack a 'historic win' for the 'Palestinian resistance'; the campus chapter at Tufts University praised the atrocities as a 'historic attack on the colonizers' to 'take back stolen land'; the chapter at George Washington University projected the words 'Glory to Our Martyrs' on the campus library; Brandeis University permanently banned the group for openly supporting Hamas; and Columbia University suspended the group for expressing 'threatening rhetoric and intimidation.'[14] Echoing Ghazi Hamad, students at university campuses on the East and West coasts of the United States chanted that 'resistance is justified' and called to 'globalize the intifada.'[15] 'On campus chat platforms,' declared an open letter signed by more than 600 Jewish students and alumni at the Ivy League Brown University, 'we have seen calls for Israeli Jews to "go back to Europe" and claims that "there is no such thing as an innocent Israeli."'[16] In this environment, not only Israeli but Jewish university students have experienced threats and in some instances violence.[17]

Reactions on my own campus were not as egregious as those reported elsewhere, but they too evinced a disturbing indifference to and lack of empathy for the victims of October 7 and hostility to Jewish students. An online petition entitled 'Sociologists in Solidarity with Gaza and the Palestinian People' condemned the 'Israeli regime' for the 'murder,' 'genocide,' and 'ethnic cleansing' of 'the Palestinian people in Gaza and the West Bank.' The petition neither condemned the atrocities committed by Hamas on October 7 nor called for the release of the hostages that Hamas abducted and held. It was signed by several colleagues and doctoral students in my department. Members of my labor union demanded endorsement of resolutions that condemned Israel in similar terms without condemning Hamas or calling for the release of hostages. I witnessed a student rally on campus at which speakers called for the 'liberation of Palestine by any means necessary,' including, presumably, the atrocities committed on October 7. During an aggressive protest in front of Hillel, the campus organization for Jewish students, the local police were called to ensure safety and escort students into the building. On November 7, Jewish students leaving a peaceful vigil to mark the one-month anniversary of the Hamas terrorist attacks in Israel were verbally harassed, and an object was thrown at them.[18]

These types of reactions to the October 7th pogrom have created deep anxiety among American Jews, who are among the most consistently liberal and Democratic groups in the US population.[19] About two weeks after the pogrom, *The New York Times* reported, 'Progressive Jews who have spent years supporting ... causes on the American left—including opposing Israeli policies in Gaza and the West Bank—are suddenly feeling abandoned by those who[m] they long thought of as allies.'[20] Dismay has led to unsettling questions. 'How,' Chemerinsky asks, 'can anyone celebrate ... the brutal massacre' of more than a thousand people or 'the pulling of people from their houses to take as hostages? If this happened to people who were not Jews, would there be such celebrations?'[21] I found myself asking similar questions and looking for insight in the scholarship that I was teaching and discussing with students in my course on the history of antisemitism. While nearly all this scholarship was helpful in one way or another for understanding the reaction to October 7, it was Jean-Paul Sartre's 1946 essay *Anti-Semite and Jew* to which my own thinking repeatedly returned.

Antisemitism, Sartre explains, is 'at bottom a form of Manichaeism. It explains the course of the world by the struggle of the principle of Good with the principle of Evil. Between these two principles no reconciliation is conceivable; one of them must triumph and the other be annihilated.'[22] The antisemite does not see a 'conflict of interests between human groups' but only 'the damage which an evil power causes society.'[23] The conflict is thus 'raised to a religious plane, and the end of the combat can be nothing other than a holy destruction.'[24] Writing less than a week after the October 7th pogrom, the American author Gal Beckerman described how such Manichaeism structured reactions to those atrocities. Many people on the left, he wrote, whom he thought would care about the suffering and 'common humanity' of the victims, could only see what had happened through 'established categories of colonized and colonizer, evil Israeli and righteous Palestinian.' They could neither recognize the moral abomination facing them nor see the 'world of Jewish suffering' in which Beckerman found himself because 'Jewish suffering simply didn't fit anywhere for them.' As Beckerman observes with painful but unflinching clarity, 'they were so set in their categories that they couldn't make a distinction between the Palestinian people and a genocidal cult that claimed to speak in that people's name. And they couldn't acknowledge hundreds and hundreds of senseless deaths because the people who were killed were Israelis and therefore the enemy.'[25] This Manichaean reaction suggests a new form of what the historian Saul Friedländer called 'redemptive antisemitism,' one that substitutes anti-colonialism for racial antisemitism but retains a quasi-religious vision of redemption understood as 'liberation from the Jews—as their expulsion, possibly their annihilation.'[26]

Sartre is not the only author to observe the Manichaean nature of antisemitism, but he goes further by exploring the psychological advantages that Manichaeism gives to the antisemite. 'Above all,' he suggests, this 'naïve dualism' is reassuring to the antisemite because it relieves him of the burden of moral reflection. 'His business is with Evil'; he is absorbed in the task of unmasking, denouncing, and eliminating it. But 'if all he has to do is to remove Evil,' Sartre writes, 'that means that the Good is already *given*. He has no need to seek it in anguish, to invent it, to scrutinize it patiently when he has found it, to prove it in action, to verify it by its consequences, or, finally, to shoulder the responsibilities of the moral choice he has made.'[27] The antisemite has no need for any of this because he expects the good to take care of itself 'when he has fulfilled his mission as holy destroyer.'[28] This attitude was apparent to me in the hostile reactions of fellow union members when I proposed to rewrite their resolutions to emphasize the things that the union believes in (human rights, international law, the protection of civilians) rather than the evils they were eager to castigate. One need not accept all the tenets of Sartrean existentialism to acknowledge that the appeal of antisemitism partly lies in the escape it offers from moral choice and responsibility.

This evasion of moral choice and responsibility is evident in other ways as well. The historian Shulamit Volkov has shown how in Wilhelmine Germany antisemitism became a cultural code, an element of a broader worldview that it symbolized and denoted. Thus, 'professing antisemitism became a sign of cultural identity, of one's belonging to a specific cultural camp,' a 'shorthand label for an entire set of ideas and attitudes having little if anything to do with direct affection or dislike of Jews.'[29] More recently, the anthropologist Sina Arnold has suggested that antizionism functions in an analogous way as a cultural code for much of the contemporary left.[30] This explains, for example, the absurdity of activists who invoke their concern for LGBTQ+ rights to account for their rejection of Israel and implicit support of Hamas.[31] Antizionism signals their membership in the community of the good, while antisemitism does little to damage their reputation as long as 'it can plausibly appear supportive of the Palestinians.'[32] In this way, some activists become what Sartre called 'secondhand anti-Semites.'[33] The point is that when antizionism becomes 'a plank in the platform,' it means that activists have 'learned to see things unreflectingly, through ready-made thought models.'[34] We have entered the realm of what Max Horkheimer and Theodor Adorno called 'ticket thinking' or a 'ticket mentality,' the defining feature of which is 'abstention from thought.'[35]

Another psychological advantage that Manichaeism affords the antisemite is that it allows him to indulge his own attraction toward evil. 'What [the antisemite] wishes, what he prepares, is the death of the Jew.'[36] Of course, praising or defending the atrocities committed on October 7 is not the same as perpetrating them, and antisemitism is not always expressed in violence. But even when antisemitism falls short of violence, it aims at the abasement, humiliation, and banishment of Jews. Chemerinsky, for example, relates how a student told him in a public forum that 'what would make her feel safe in the [University of California Berkeley] law school would be "to get rid of the Zionists."'[37] These measures, as Sartre astutely observes, are 'symbolic murders,' substitutes for real murders such as those that Hamas committed on October 7.[38] Manichaeism licenses the expression of this murderous impulse insofar as the antisemite sees himself as a 'criminal in a good cause' who therefore has 'conscience on his side.' 'Here again,' Sartre points out, 'he flees responsibilities .... He knows that he is wicked, but since he does Evil for the sake of Good, since a whole people waits for deliverance at his hands, he looks upon himself as a sanctified evildoer. By a sort of inversion of all values, … the anti-Semite accords esteem, respect, and enthusiasm to anger, hate, pillage, murder, to all the forms of violence.'[39] Moreover, Sartre observes, the antisemite can 'glut himself to the point of obsession with the recital of obscene or criminal actions which excite and satisfy his perverse leanings; but since at the same time he attributes them to those infamous Jews on whom he heaps his scorn, he satisfies himself without being compromised.'[40] We see this not only in lurid recitals of the crimes that Israelis are accused of perpetrating against the Palestinians—including, a Maryland school teacher declared, organ theft—but also in bizarre accusations that Israelis are themselves responsible for the atrocities committed on October 7.[41] As Sartre acknowledges, this aspect of his analysis relies on the Freudian concept of projection—the unconscious transfer of one's own desires or emotions to another person—which has long been central to psychoanalytic explanations of antisemitism. And what is projection if not a means of evading responsibility?

Every discussion of antisemitism eventually invites the question, what is to be done? The answer that Sartre gave in 1946 is profoundly problematic. One expects him to find the remedy to antisemitism in his own existentialist philosophy, which emphasizes the unavoidable necessity of making choices and the grave moral responsibility that freedom and choice entail. Sartre does indeed urge his Jewish readers to respond to antisemitism in what he calls an authentic way: to choose oneself as Jew rather than to deny or flee from the situation in which one is thrown.[42] But Sartre maintains that such authenticity is not a social or political solution to antisemitism.[43] Where, then, does the solution lie? In the end, Sartre falls back on the well-worn orthodox Marxist answer to the Jewish question: class struggle, revolution, and ultimately assimilation.[44] Ironically, Sartre proposes the very thing the antisemite desires but cannot achieve: the banishment of the Jew as Jew. It was an answer that Sartre could offer without qualms because he denied any positive or substantive content to Jewishness that one might wish to preserve. If the antisemite makes the Jew, as he famously declared, then the Jew is nothing more than a by product of the hatred one seeks to abolish. Such an answer can only satisfy readers who see Jewishness as something to be shed or transcended. For the rest of us, the only convincing answers that Jews have ever found to antisemitism are, first, open and liberal societies in which Jews can survive and flourish as Jews, and second, a homeland that provides a haven for Jewish refugees and their descendants and enables Jews to defend themselves.[45] We find little reason in the long history of antisemitism or in its current resurgence to doubt the necessity of these answers.

Notes

1 Fabian, E. and Pacchiani, G. (2023) 'IDF estimates 3,000 Hamas terrorists invaded Israel in Oct. 7 onslaught', *Times of Israel*, 1 November. Available at: https://www.timesofisrael.com/idf-estimates-3000-hamas-terrorists-invaded-israel-in-oct-7-onslaught/ (Accessed: 3 January 2024).

2 Lankford, J. *et al.* (2023) Letter from J. Lankford and 33 other US senators to US Ambassador to the United Nations L. Thomas-Greenfield, 9 November. Available at: https://www.lankford.senate.gov/wp-content/uploads/2023/11/Lankford-Rosen-Letter-to-UN.pdf (Accessed: 3 January 2024).

3 Hoffman, B. (2023) 'Understanding Hamas's genocidal ideology', *The Atlantic*, 10 October. Available at: https://www.theatlantic.com/international/archive/2023/10/hamas-covenant-israel-attack-war-genocide/675602/ (Accessed: 3 January 2024).

4 Winer, S. (2023) 'Hamas actions are war crimes, could constitute genocide – international law experts', *Times of Israel*, 15 October. Available at: https://www.timesofisrael.com/hamas-actions-are-war-crimes-could-constitute-genocide-international-law-experts/ (Accessed: 3 January 2024).

5 Pacchiani, G. and Bachner, M. (2023) 'Hamas official says group aims to repeat Oct. 7 onslaught many times to destroy Israel', *Times of Israel*, 1 November. Available at: https://www.timesofisrael.com/hamas-official-says-group-aims-to-repeat-oct-7-onslaught-many-times-to-destroy-israel/ (Accessed: 3 January 2024).

6 Baker, P. (2023) 'In unforgiving terms, Biden condemns "evil" and "abhorrent" attack on Israel', *New York Times*, 10 October. Available at: https://www.nytimes.com/2023/10/10/us/politics/biden-israel-hamas.html (Accessed: 3 January 2024). Agence France-Presse. (2023) 'EU chief Von der Leyen says Hamas attack an "act of war" that reflects "an ancient evil"', *Times of Israel*, 11 October. Available at: https://www.timesofisrael.com/liveblog_entry/eu-chief-von-der-leyen-says-hamas-attack-an-act-of-war-that-reflects-an-ancient-evil/ (Accessed: 3 January 2024).

7 Medina, J. and Lerer, L. (2023) 'On Israel, progressive Jews feel abandoned by their left-wing allies', *New York Times*, 20 October. Available at: https://www.nytimes.com/2023/10/20/us/politics/progressive-jews-united-states.html (Accessed: 3 January 2024).

8 Anti-Defamation League. (2023) 'Fringe-left groups express support for Hamas's invasion and brutal attacks in Israel', 14 October. Available at: https://www.adl.org/resources/blog/fringe-left-groups-express-support-hamass-invasion-and-brutal-attacks-israel (Accessed: 3 January 2024). Gergely, J. (2023) 'Rep. Alexandria Ocasio-Cortez condemns pro-Palestinian rally in Times Square', *NY Jewish Week*, 10 October. Available at: https://www.jta.org/2023/10/10/ny/rep-alexandria-ocasio-cortez-condemns-pro-palestine-rally-in-times-square (Accessed: 3 January 2024).

9 Propper, D. (2023) 'NYC DSA apologizes for promoting pro-Palestinian rally—but doesn't condemn Hamas', *New York Post*, 10 October. Available at: https://nypost.com/2023/10/10/nyc-dsa-apologizes-for-promoting-pro-palestinian-rally-but-doesnt-condemn-hamas/ (Accessed: 3 January 2024).

10 European Union of Jewish Students. (2023) 'The rise of antisemitic acts and incidents in universities across Europe since 7th of October 2023', 6 November. Available at: https://eujs.org/resources/antisemitism/report-rise-of-antisemitic-acts-and-incidents-in-universities-across-europe-since-7th-of-october-2023/ (Accessed: 3 January 2024).

11 Pagano, J.-P. (2023) 'Macroaggression', *All the Apparatus* (blog), 15 October. Available at: https://johnpaulpagano.substack.com/p/macroaggression (Accessed: 3 January 2024).

12 Chemerinsky, E. (2023) 'Nothing has prepared me for the antisemitism I see on college campuses now', *Los Angeles Times*, 29 October. Available at: https://www.latimes.com/opinion/story/2023-10-29/antisemitism-college-campus-israel-hamas-palestine (Accessed: 3 January 2024). Massad, J. (2023) 'Just another battle or the Palestinian war of liberation?' *The Electronic Intifada*, 8 October. Available at: https://electronicintifada.net/content/just-another-battle-or-palestinian-war-liberation/38661 (Accessed: 3 January 2024). Fenster, J. N. (2023)

'Petition calls for Yale professor's removal after making posts about Hamas attack on Israel', *CT Insider*, 12 October. Available at: https://www.ctinsider.com/connecticut/article/yale-petition-israel-antisemetic-removal-18421892.php (Accessed: 3 January 2024). Walker, J. (2023) 'Chicago art professor under fire for calling Israelis "irredeemable excrement" in wake of Hamas invasion', *The National Desk*, 18 October. Available at: https://thenationaldesk.com/news/americas-news-now/chicago-art-professor-under-fire-for-calling-israelis-irredeemable-excrement-in-wake-of-hamas-invasion-school-institute-mika-tosca-israel-palestine-terrorism-terrorist-middle-east-conflict-chicago-illinois (Accessed: 3 January 2024). Childs, J. (2023) 'UC Davis condemns post apparently by professor threatening "zionist journalists"', *Los Angeles Times*, 21 October. Available at: https://www.latimes.com/california/story/2023-10-21/uc-davis-condemns-post-apparently-by-professsor-threatening-zionist-journalists (Accessed: 3 January 2024).

13 Hill, J. S. and Orakwue, N. L. (2023) 'Harvard student groups face intense backlash for statement calling Israel "entirely responsible" for Hamas attack', *Harvard Crimson*, 10 October. Available at: https://www.thecrimson.com/article/2023/10/10/psc-statement-backlash/ (Accessed: 3 January 2024).

14 National Students for Justice in Palestine. (2023) 'Day of resistance toolkit', n.d. Available at: https://dw-wp-production.imgix.net/2023/10/DAY-OF-RESISTANCE-TOOLKIT.pdf (Accessed: 3 January 2024). Vos, D. (2023) 'University denounces SJP praise of Hamas-led attacks', *The Tufts Daily*, 12 October. Available at: https://www.tuftsdaily.com/article/2023/10/university-denounces-sjp-praise-of-hamas-led-attacks (Accessed: 3 January 2024). Hajdenberg, J. (2023) 'Students for Justice in Palestine suspended at George Washington University, adding to a growing trend', *Jewish Telegraphic Agency*, 15 November. Available at: https://www.jta.org/2023/11/15/united-states/students-for-justice-in-palestine-suspended-at-george-washington-university-adding-to-a-growing-trend (Accessed: 3 January 2024).

15 Edwards, J. and Ostadan, B. (2023) 'Protests erupt at NYC colleges responding to Israel-Hamas war', *Gothamist*, 12 October. Available at: https://gothamist.com/news/protests-erupt-at-nyc-colleges-responding-to-israel-hamas-war (Accessed: 3 January 2024). Bradley, D., Feld, A. K. and King, S. (2023) 'Reed College protest ends in four student arrests, demonstrators chant "globalize the intifada"', *Quest*, 11 November. Available at: https://reedquest.org/2023/11/11/reed-college-protest-ends-in-four-student-arrests-demonstrators-chant-globalize-the-intifada/ (Accessed: 3 January 2024).

16 Lederman, J. *et al.* (2023) 'An open letter in support of Israel, from Jewish students and alumni at Brown University', *Brown Daily Herald*, 15 November. Available at: https://www.browndailyherald.com/article/2023/11/an-open-letter-in-support-of-israel-from-jewish-students-and-alumni-at-brown-university (Accessed: 3 January 2024).

17 Sokol, S. (2023) 'Jewish students in the U.K. face "over a year's worth of antisemitic incidents" in a month', *Haaretz*, 8 November. Available at: https://www.haaretz.com/world-news/europe/2023-11-08/ty-article/.premium/jewish-students-in-the-u-k-face-over-a-years-worth-of-antisemitic-incidents-in-a-month/0000018b-aff0-dedf-adab-eff04f440000 (Accessed: 3 January 2024). WABC-TV New York (2023) 'Teen charged after attacking student hanging pro-Israel posters at Columbia University', 16 October. Available at: https://abc7ny.com/nyc-columbia-university-israel-war/13914229/ (Accessed: 3 January 2024).

18 Beran, L. (2023) 'Madison police investigate rock thrown at students after pro-Israel vigil', *Daily Cardinal*, 9 November. Available at: https://www.dailycardinal.com/article/2023/11/madison-police-investigate-rock-thrown-at-students-after-pro-israel-vigil (Accessed: 3 January 2024).

19 Pew Research Center. (2021) 'Jewish Americans in 2020', 11 May, pp. 159–169. Available at: https://www.pewresearch.org/religion/2021/05/11/u-s-jews-political-views/ (Accessed: 3 January 2024).

20 Medina, J. and Lerer, L. (2023) 'On Israel, progressive Jews feel abandoned by their left-wing allies', *New York Times*, 20 October. Available at: https://www.nytimes.com/2023/10/20/us/politics/progressive-jews-united-states.html (Accessed: 3 January 2024).

21 Chemerinsky, E. (2023) 'Nothing has prepared me for the antisemitism I see on college campuses now', *Los Angeles Times*, 29 October. Available at: https://www.latimes.com/opinion/story/2023-10-29/antisemitism-college-campus-israel-hamas-palestine (Accessed: 3 January 2024).

22 Sartre, J.-P. ([1948] 1976) *Anti-Semite and Jew*. Translated by G. J. Becker. New York: Schocken, pp. 40–41.

23 Sartre, J.-P. ([1948] 1976) *Anti-Semite and Jew*. Translated by G. J. Becker. New York: Schocken, pp. 42–43.

24 Sartre, J.-P. ([1948] 1976) *Anti-Semite and Jew*. Translated by G. J. Becker. New York: Schocken, p. 43.

25 Beckerman, G. (2023) 'The left abandoned me', *The Atlantic*, 12 October. Available at: https://www.theatlantic.com/ideas/archive/2023/10/left-jewish-suffering-israel-hamas/675621/ (Accessed: 3 January 2024).

26 Friedländer, S. (1997) *Nazi Germany and the Jews*, Vol. 1: *The years of persecution, 1933–1939*. New York: Harper Collins, pp. 73–112. Quotation from p. 87.

27 Sartre, J.-P. ([1948] 1976) *Anti-Semite and Jew*. Translated by G. J. Becker. New York: Schocken, pp. 44–45.

28 Sartre, J.-P. ([1948] 1976) *Anti-Semite and Jew*. Translated by G. J. Becker. New York: Schocken, p. 45.

29 Volkov, S. (1978) 'Antisemitism as a cultural code: reflections on the history and historiography of antisemitism in Imperial Germany', *Leo Baeck Institute Yearbook* 23(1), pp. 25–46. Quotation from pp. 34–35.

30 Arnold, S. (2015) 'From occupation to occupy: antisemitism and the contemporary left in the United States', in Rosenfeld, A. H. (ed.) *Deciphering the new antisemitism*. Bloomington: Indiana University Press, pp. 375–404. On antizionism as a cultural code, see pp. 391–392, 394.

31 Binion, B. (2023) 'The contradictions of "queers for Palestine"', *Reason*, 27 October. Available at: https://reason.com/2023/10/27/the-contradictions-of-queers-for-palestine/ (Accessed: 3 January 2024). Lewis, H. (2023) 'The progressives who flunked the Hamas test', *The Atlantic*, 13 October. Available at: https://www.theatlantic.com/ideas/archive/2023/10/hamas-pop-intersectionality-leftism-israel/675625/ (Accessed: 3 January 2024). Navabi, A. (2023) 'Queers for Palestine: identity politics at its most absurd', *Quillette*, 2 November. Available at: https://quillette.com/2023/11/02/queers-for-palestine/ (Accessed: 3 January 2024).

32 Hirsh, D. (2017) *Contemporary left antisemitism*. New York: Routledge, p. 52.

33 Sartre, J.-P. ([1948] 1976) *Anti-Semite and Jew*. Translated by G. J. Becker. New York: Schocken, p. 52.

34 Horkheimer, M. and Adorno, T. W. ([1947] 2020) *Dialectic of enlightenment*. Translated by E. Jephcott. Stanford: Stanford University Press, pp. 166–167.

35 Horkheimer, M. and Adorno, T. W. ([1947] 2020) *Dialectic of enlightenment*. Translated by E. Jephcott. Stanford: Stanford University Press, pp. 170–172.

36 Sartre, J.-P. ([1948] 1976) *Anti-Semite and Jew*. Translated by G. J. Becker. New York: Schocken, p. 49.

37 Chemerinsky, E. (2023) 'Nothing has prepared me for the antisemitism I see on college campuses now', *Los Angeles Times*, 29 October. Available at: https://www.latimes.com/opinion/story/2023-10-29/antisemitism-college-campus-israel-hamas-palestine (Accessed: 3 January 2024).

38 Sartre, J.-P. ([1948] 1976) *Anti-Semite and Jew*. Translated by G. J. Becker. New York: Schocken, p. 49.

39 Sartre, J.-P. ([1948] 1976) *Anti-Semite and Jew*. Translated by G. J. Becker. New York: Schocken, pp. 49–50.

40 Sartre, J.-P. ([1948] 1976) *Anti-Semite and Jew*. Translated by G. J. Becker. New York: Schocken, p. 46.

41 Asbury, N. (2023) 'Montgomery teacher denies Hamas raid, accuses Israel of organ theft', *Washington Post*, 16 November. Available at: https://www.washingtonpost.com/education/2023/11/15/antisemitism-montgomery-county-teacher/ (Accessed: 3 January 2024). Pacchiani, G. (2023) 'PA falsely says Oct. 7 rave massacre was committed by IDF; Netanyahu: preposterous', *Times of Israel*, 19 November. Available at: https://www.timesofisrael.com/pa-falsely-says-oct-7-rave-massacre-was-committed-by-idf-netanyahu-preposterous/ (Accessed: 3 January 2024). Weinstein, N. (2023) 'Oakland City Council rejects bid to denounce Hamas as public speakers lacerate Israel', *Jewish Telegraphic Agency*, 29 November. Available at: https://www.jta.org/2023/11/29/united-states/oakland-city-council-rejects-bid-to-denounce-hamas-as-public-speakers-lacerate-israel (Accessed: 3 January 2024).

42 Sartre, J.-P. ([1948] 1976) *Anti-Semite and Jew*. Translated by G. J. Becker. New York: Schocken, pp. 136–137.

43 Sartre, J.-P. ([1948] 1976) *Anti-Semite and Jew*. Translated by G. J. Becker. New York: Schocken, p. 141.

44 Sartre, J.-P. ([1948] 1976) *Anti-Semite and Jew*. Translated by G. J. Becker. New York: Schocken, pp. 149–151.

45 Lappin, S. (2019) 'The re-emergence of the Jewish question', *Journal of Contemporary Antisemitism*, 2(1), pp. 29–46.

3 The Rise and Rise of the 'Israel Question'

Daniel Chernilo

On Saturday 11 November 2023, which marked Armistice Day in the UK, an estimated 500,000 people descended on Central London to protest against Israel's war against Hamas in Gaza. This was the biggest anti-war demonstration in the country for 20 years – the last one having taken place in February 2003 to oppose Tony Blair's decision to back the US attempt to topple Iraq's dictator Saddam Hussein. The only comparable political rally in the UK's recent history was a march of about a million people to demand a fresh Brexit referendum, in October 2019. While the anger and emotions triggered by the Iraq War and Brexit may be accounted for by the combination of domestic issues and the UK's international standing, little of what has been taking place in Israel or Gaza has much to do with UK internal politics nor does it have a direct bearing on Britain's international agenda. Indeed, given that the terrorist attacks by Hamas on Israel on 7 October did not elicit much sympathy within UK civil society, it is clear that Israeli misdeeds produce a very particular kind of moral wrath and political mobilisation.

Possible explanations for this situation will necessarily remain contested and may include the history of Britain's muddled imperial politics in the Middle East in the first half of the twentieth century as well as greater Muslim presence within British society after that. But even as sympathy for Palestinian suffering is to be expected on the face of the enormous human toll of the conflict, the level and intensity of anti-Israel rhetoric raises some difficult questions. On the one hand, antipathy to Israel often takes the unique form of questioning its very right to exist; on the other hand, diaspora Jews living anywhere in the world are treated as 'proxy Israelis' and thus as legitimate recipients of local hostility because of Israeli actions. The net effect is that the crimes perpetrated against Israelis in Israel, as those of Hamas on 7 October, as well as the harassment Jews experience elsewhere in the world, are explained away as regrettable yet understandable reactions to Israel's policies against the Palestinians. Israel is held responsible not only for its own actions but also for *other people's hatred towards its citizens and Jews worldwide*. The common antisemitic trope that Jews are the main cause of their own misery is as alive today as it has ever been.

DOI: 10.4324/9781003497424-3

The main issue that I would like to explore in this chapter is that the shape of the unique positioning of *Israel* within contemporary, global, civil society echoes the ways in which *Jews* were once positioned, as they aspired to equality within national societies, in Europe, at the end of the eighteenth century. In other words, it looks like *the 'Israel question', in its current manifestations is a twenty-first century incarnation of earlier 'Jewish questions'*. In order to substantiate this claim, I will proceed in three steps, which in turn make up the structure of this chapter. I start off by recounting how and why the raising of various such 'questions' became a powerful rhetorical and political device at the time of the formation of European nation-states since the Enlightenment. I will locate debates on the 'Jewish question' within that framework (the 'The Jews in the Age of (National) Questions' section). I then show how, as global trends have become increasingly salient in the past 50 years, this way of thinking has also become the standard way of grappling with the international standing of the Jewish state (the 'Israel and the International Jewish Question' section). I finish with the thesis that, whether as a 'national Jewish question' or an 'international Israel question', similar antisemitic tropes are being mobilised (the 'The Antisemitism Question. Then and Now' section).

The Jews in the Age of (National) Questions

In her recent book, *The Age of Questions*, Holly Case analyses the rise of a powerful new rhetorical device which, since the late eighteenth century, has become a common feature of novel European national polities and public spheres.[1] Polemicists of various ilk started raising a number of different 'questions' which, as they saw them, constituted the most fundamental challenge of their times. While ostensibly concerned with *particular* topics and subject groups – from Jews and women to tuberculosis and war – awareness of their unique importance vis-à-vis the future of society carried a message of *universal significance*. Whatever their subjects or topics, these questions were seen as the main challenge societies needed to overcome; they were the main obstacle between a deficient status quo in need of urgent resolution and a future condition of social and political emancipation. These questions were all raised in the name of progressive politics and the very resistance to recognising their salience was understood as a conservative defect that hampered attempts at enlightened social reform. Furthermore, most of these 'questions' were concerned directly with the changing nature of the relations between domestic and international politics in European states: whether and how different ethnic groups were able to mobilise their claims to cultural and even political autonomy vis-à-vis traditional forms of state authority based on kingship, lineage and religion. In Case's account, there are two additional features that were characteristic of the way these questions were commonly raised: first, the populations involved needed to be willing to partake in the solution to their own situation; otherwise, they would themselves be to blame in the continuation of their afflictions. Second, as these were practical rather than theoretical questions, they did not demand so much *answers* as definitive, indeed final, *solutions*.

This was already the intellectual environment within which Moses Mendelssohn (1729–1786), the doyen of the Jewish Enlightenment, had to react when challenged to explain how, given his preference for modern philosophy and science, he nonetheless decided to hold on to his ostensibly irrational religious faith. Mendelssohn's answer to this Jewish question, most explicit in his book *Jerusalem* of 1783, is not only a defence of Judaism but a refusal of the very terms within which anti-Jewish polemics were already being raised: he rejected the premiss that there was something intrinsically un-enlightened in Judaism as this betrayed his opponents' deficient knowledge of, or indeed bad faith against, Judaism itself.[2] By the time of Karl Marx's famous engagement with Bruno Bauer in the 1840s, the 'Jewish question' was well rooted inside the universe of progressive politics.[3] Both Bauer and Marx understood that the successful resolution of the 'Jewish question' was dependent upon both parties – Germans as much as Jews – being able to move with the times, they had to open themselves to social and political reform and leave their old prejudices behind. In the specific case of the Jewish question, however, the additional complication was that it involved not only a resolution regarding their future social and legal standing in Germany but a definitive answer to the question of whether Jews were a religious group, a nation or even a 'race'. This needed permanent elucidation because it was thought an essential element to finally explain the most troubling features of Jewish life: why have the Jews remained committed to laws and precepts whose strictures tend to keep them apart from other groups? Is their religious sense of chosenness compatible with a commitment to national integration under the principle of equality before the law? Can Jews ever become fully-fledged citizens of their 'host' countries without surrendering their Jewish identities? Crucially, answers to these questions were themselves predicated on the fact that the root causes of the antipathy Jews inevitably generate are their own fault. Was there anything that that Jews themselves ought to do to overcome antisemitism and become worthy of civic integration within modern nations?[4]

This intrinsically antisemitic framework of the Jewish question is well established: it is never a Jewish question but always, in effect, an antisemitism question.[5] But one aspect worthy of mention is that the rise of political Zionism in the late nineteenth century took place well *after* debates on the Jewish question had been established within those terms. As an indigenous Jewish response to the failures of previous solutions to the Jewish question, the rise of Jewish nationalism also offered the opportunity to reinforce those very prejudices. At least one consequence of Jews starting to frame their own politics in national terms was that to argue that they appeared to be *willingly giving up* on the promise of national integration *within Europe*. Indeed, this raised the stakes even further, because now the achievement of political autonomy required their migration to a land that they could claim as their own.[6] Zionism was both a local and a global movement that, as it challenged the terms through which the Jewish question had been framed for most of the previous century, also transferred it onto the international arena. The Zionist response appeared to reinforce the view that, as Jews themselves had now admitted they were alien and foreign in Europe, the success or indeed failure of their attempt at national normalisation *in Palestine* was to become the new litmus test on which it rested their traditional status as the West's universal scapegoat.

Israel and the International Jewish Question

In the aftermath of World War II and the Holocaust, the establishment of the State of Israel in 1948 appeared, initially at least, to mark a turning point in the antisemitic undertones of the Jewish question of the nineteenth century. On the one side, Jew-hatred could arguably descend no further into the abyss than the pure evil of the Nazis and their success in realising it in the world; on the other hand, Jews themselves had at long last succeeded in holding their national destiny in their own hands. The foundation of Israel offered the opportunity to put an end to Jewish exceptionalism: Jews were now, unequivocally, a nation like all others because they have a state of their own. Counting on the good will, albeit not the explicit support, of a great deal of the international community, the only explicit opposition the establishment of the new state had to overcome at the time came from its Arab neighbours. The democratic and socialist leanings of the early Zionist leadership that governed the country during its first decades also helped make Israel's initial years look like a nation-state like any other. Even with regard to questions of internal minorities and the securing of external borders against unwelcoming neighbours, Israel did look – for a short while at least – as if it was a somewhat unremarkable country.

Things started to change in the early 1970s, however. For Israel, the Yom Kippur War in October 1973 marked a turning point. On the one hand, there was a growing international assessment that, as it eventually defeated the Arab states' surprising invasion, Israel had become an expansionist country bent on annihilating its neighbours; on the other, within Israel itself, there was the increasing political role played by the right-wing 'revisionist' Zionism. This new portrayal of the Jewish state that started to emerge made its previous normalcy short-lived. Israel was now widely caste as a bastion of Western colonial power in a predominately post-colonial setting; it was the result of a brutal settler mentality that had become organised around the persecution and eventual 'genocide' of the Palestinian population. As it turned 25 years of age, Israel was already seen as a country *unlike* any other.[7] By 1975, even the UN had passed its famous 3379 resolution that Zionism was a form of racism: as the shouting of 'dirty Jew' was by now inextricably associated with Nazism, it was now tempting to add not 'dirty' but 'racist', to the word 'Zionist'.

Crucially, geopolitical changes in the Middle East coincided with the beginning of the end of the Vietnam War (1955–1975), which not only unified internal dissidents inside the US against the country's neo-imperialist foreign policy but was also able to unify progressive politics worldwide under the rhetoric of 'anti-imperialism'. As opposition to the Vietnam War came to symbolise an early *global* consciousness of this new variant of 'anti-imperialism', this coincided with separation of Palestinian interest from the interests of Arabs as a whole, the creation of the Palestinian Liberation Organisation, and the emergence of its main leader, Yasser Arafat. By the end of the 1970s, the Palestinian had become the world's most symbolic anti-imperialist struggle; not so much because of the legitimacy or otherwise of its claims but because dislike of Israel was the only thing on which this branch of Western anti-imperialism and the official international politics of the Soviet Union were able to agree. By the time of the fall of the Berlin War and the end of communism, in 1990, and with greater intensity with the collapse of the Oslo peace process towards the end of the 1990s, the early national Jewish question had definitively mutated into the international Israel question: the question about the Jews' (un)willingness and (in)ability to integrate fully and in good faith into the respective national polities of their host countries was transformed into Israel's (un)willingness and (in)ability to integrate fully and in good faith into the international community by holding itself accountable to the standards of international law. To the same degree that the early 'Jewish question' was really an antisemitism question, the contemporary 'Israel question' is also an antisemitism one: it demonises the actions of the Jewish state because it is Jewish, regards them as criminal beyond redemption because it is a Jewish state, and holds Israel accountable to a different standard vis-à-vis other states.

The Antisemitism Question: Then and Now

Among its many flaws, this account of the Israel question overlooks the fact that over the past 250 years, most if not all modern states have consolidated their territory through morally 'objectionable' means vis-à-vis their neighbours and minorities. In the US, Australia and throughout Europe, in China, India and all over Latin America, modern states have systematically resorted to the use of violence and have justified it in terms of securing national self-determination. Rather than understanding Zionism as yet another form of nationalism – as problematic and normatively ambivalent as all nationalisms are[8] – what could and should have remained within the confines of a *political* critique of state action went as far as questioning Israel's right to exist. Israel's wrongdoings were essentialised as being the somewhat inevitable result of its uniquely sinful origin. What had initially emerged as a main anomaly within Jewish life – Zionism as the secular ideology of Jewish *national* 'rebirth' – became integrated into the overarching narratives of previous Jewish questions.

Zionism has now been definitively reframed within the confines of traditional antisemitic tropes of Jewish obduracy, duplicity chauvinism and misanthropy.

Three additional factors contributed to creating the ideological battleground that appear to give credence to the antisemitic double-standards against which Israel's policies are constantly criticised. First, as mentioned, the use of 'Zionist' as an expletive increasingly replaced earlier negative uses of 'the Jews', which had become associated too closely with openly racist views. In turn, this allowed left-wing anti-Zionism not only to disguise its antisemitism but to convince itself that there was absolutely nothing in their critique of Israel that echoed the twentieth-century antisemitic rhetoric of ring-wing totalitarianism.[9] Second, in the majority of the Western world, but particularly in the US, for the generation born after the 1960s Jews were no longer perceived as an ethnic minority or a group that had been subject to systematic mistreatment and discrimination; rather the opposite, Jews became 'white' insofar as their social and economic capital is concerned. Israel could be distrusted *because* it is the state of the Jews (who can never be trusted) and, as Israelis and Jews alike are now construed as 'white', the intersectional solidarities that are afforded to other 'subaltern' groups become suspended in their case. Finally, diaspora Jews could again be treated as a foreign 'national' minority vis-à-vis their connection to Israel as the homeland of 'all' Jews. However long Jewish communities had lived in various countries, it became possible for them to be treated as (more or less) tolerated denizens rather than fully-fledged citizens.

The legitimacy of the Palestinians is not under question nor is expression of solidarity for their national pledge. Yet the terms and practical implications of much of what takes place within the international alliance that lends it support has had less to do with the success of Palestinian demands than with a delegitimisation of Israel that is couched within the antisemitic premisses of the Jewish question. Then as well as now, Jews (Zionists, Israelis) are portrayed as a group who care about nothing but themselves, their current military hubris being just a secular variation of their religious sense of being the chosen people. Their newly found nationalism is the most fanatic the world has ever witnessed and whatever motives or goals Jews may openly declare, there is always a hidden agenda behind them. Whatever allegiances Jews may be able to forge, they are always made in bad faith and Zionists will turn them into their immoral goals. Needless to say, Jews will have no shame even in exaggerating the crimes to which they have victim if this allows them to commit those very crimes themselves.

Closing Remarks

Over the past 200 years, one of the foundational questions of modern European states has been that of what to do with the Jews. Specific concerns and issues have of course varied, but the underlying frameworks within which concerns have been raised have remained within all too familiar antisemitic stereotypes. Whether Jews are seen as insufficiently German or French, Zionists as racists and Israel as a settler state, the same antisemitic prejudices of Jewish chosenness and exceptionalism are being deployed. Whatever the merits of the Palestinian cause, and there is much to support in their claim to national self-determination as part of a two-state solution, its global status as the symbol of all anti-imperialist struggles has been construed on the wrong, antisemitic premisses. Sadly, the most pressing concern in this apparent show of solidarity takes the old form of bringing the Israel question to its own radical final solution.

Notes

1 Case, Holly (2018) *The age of questions. Or, a first attempt at an aggregate history of the Eastern, social, woman, American, Jewish, Polish, bullion, tuberculosis and many other questions over the nineteenth century, and beyond* (Princeton: Princeton University Press).

2 Altman, Alexander (1983) 'Introduction', in Mendelssohn, M. *Jerusalem. Or on religious power and Judaism* (Lebanon, New Hampshire: University Press of New England).

3 Marx, Karl (1975) 'On the Jewish question', in Marx, K. *Early writings* (London: Penguin).

4 Chernilo, Daniel (2023) 'The Jews killed Moses. Sigmund Freud and the Jewish question', *Theory, Culture and Society*, https://doi.org/10.1177/02632764231201333

5 See, for instance, Dalsheim, Joyce and Starrett, Gregory (eds.) (2020) *The Jewish question again* (Chicago: Prickly Paradigm Press); Fine, Robert and Philip Spencer (2017) *Antisemitism and the left. On the return of the Jewish question* (Manchester: Manchester University Press); Lapidot, Elad (2020) *Jews out of the question. A critique of Anti-anti-semitism* (New York: Suny University Press), Roudinesco, Elisabeth (2013) *Revisiting the Jewish question* (Cambridge: Polity Press); and Nirenberg, David (2013) *Anti-Judaism. The history of a way of thinking* (New York: WW Norton).

6 This was precisely the main argument that non-Zionist Jews offered in their own rejection of a purely national solution of the Jewish problem. See Meyer, Michael (1998) *Response to modernity. A history of the reform movement in Judaism* (Detroit: Wayne State University Press).

7 Within Jewish historiography of Zionism and the foundation of Israel, this argument can be found in Mayer, Arno (2021) *Plowshares into swords. From Zionism to Israel* (London: Verso).

8 Chernilo, Daniel (2020) 'Beyond the nation? Or back to it? Current trends in the sociology of nations and nationalism', *Sociology* 54 (6): 1072–1087.

9 Wistrich, Robert (2012) *From ambivalence to betrayal. The left, the Jews and Israel* (Lincoln and London: The University of Nebraska Press).

4 Jewish 'Whiteness' and Its Effects in the Aftermath of October 7

Linda Maizels

Individuals, organizations, and governments worldwide expressed shock and horror at the brutality of the October 7 attacks, which included murder, torture, and rape. Many also voiced their outrage at another disturbing element in the aftermath of the assault: the willingness of some activists on the political left to excuse, rationalize, or even celebrate the violence perpetrated by Hamas.

Although some commentators expressed shock at the callous reaction of these activists, others emphasized the fact that the hateful reactions from some segments of the political left were not anomalous. They were a culmination of decades of animosity in some segments of the left toward Israel, which since the late 1960s has been routinely characterized as a racist, illegitimate, and colonial entity. What many of these analysts overlooked, however, was that this antagonism toward Israel was also related to a tendency by some segments of the left to express hostility toward American Jews because they were predisposed to see them as uniformly white and privileged.

In an article for *Politico*, writer Joshua Zeitz identified the aftermath of the 1967 War as a turning point in the relationship between the New Left and many American Jews because of the movement's seemingly rote hostility toward Israel and Zionism. Zeitz began by recalling the sense of 'apparent abandonment' that American Jews, particularly the wide majority of those who identified as liberals, felt in 1967 when their putative political allies 'voiced greater concern and affinity for hostile Arab countries than for the state of Israel.' He suggested that this historical feeling of abandonment intensified in the aftermath of October 7, when many on the left appeared to support or excuse what was in effect 'a modern-day pogrom that included rape, the murder of babies, the kidnapping of young and old civilians by the hundreds and gangland executions of innocents.' Zeitz continued that many American Jews 'are writhing in anger at self-styled progressives who strike them as wholly insensitive to Jewish suffering and trigger-happy not just to decry Israel's military response but to deny its very right to exist.'[1]

The commonalities that Zeitz alleged between some of the left-wing reactions after the 1967 War and October 7 would have been easily affirmed by

DOI: 10.4324/9781003497424-4

analysts writing in the immediate post-1967 era. Their books and articles confirm that many American Jews were alienated from the New Left because of the movement's opposition to Israel. However, a number of those writing in the late 1960s and early 1970s also theorized that hostility toward Israel was intimately connected to animosity directed toward Jews, whom some elements of the political left identified only as white and privileged. The sum of this hostility toward a racist, colonial Israel and a white and privileged Jewish community was a large part of what these analysts labeled 'the new antisemitism.'

In 1972, sociologist Seymour Martin Lipset criticized the automatic anti-Israel and anti-Zionist posturing espoused by much of the New Left. He assured readers that opposition to Israel and Zionism could be expressed without resorting to antisemitism but asserted that too many activists resorted to antisemitic rhetoric in their use of 'age-old hostility to Jews to strengthen a political position.' Lipset's allegations are familiar to today's analysts, who argue that many leftists resort to antisemitic allegations about Jewish power, influence, and money to express their opposition to Israel and Zionism. However, Lipset also averred that one of the most damning elements of New Left antisemitism was not 'their occasionally overt anti-Semitic statements'; rather, Lipset condemned 'the fact that they explicitly support extremist black and Arab groups who voice naked anti-Semitism.' He pointed, in particular, to the conflation of antagonism toward Jews and opposition to Israel. This meant that 'ghetto slumlords, shopkeepers, schoolteachers, the South African economic elite, [and] the owners of diamond and gold mines in black Africa' could all be condemned as 'Zionists.'[2] It is often assumed that hostility to Israel is a cause of antisemitism against diaspora Jews, but Lipset was already articulating the position that at the same time antisemitism against Jews can be a cause of hostility to Israel.

Similarly, Benjamin R. Epstein and Arnold Forster, the director and the general counsel of the Anti-Defamation League (ADL), charged, in their 1974 book *The New Anti-Semitism*, that the radical and totalitarian left represented 'a danger to world Jewry at least equal to the danger on the right.' In part, this was because less than 25 years after the genocide of European Jewry, the zero-sum game of American identity politics meant that Jews were being eclipsed as a marginalized or threatened group and were often no longer recognized as such. Instead, it was 'nonwhite Americans' who were the 'principal victim and object of concern' for the left. Consequently, according to Forster and Epstein, Jews faced, 'a large measure of indifference to the most profound apprehensions of the Jewish people; a blandness and apathy in dealing with anti-Jewish behavior; [and] a widespread incapacity or unwillingness to comprehend the necessity of the existence of Israel to Jewish safety and survival throughout the world.'[3] The two issues of Israel and American Jewish identity were seen as inextricably tied.

Analyst Earl Raab concluded in 1974 that 'increasingly, the only ethnic groups which are seen as having legitimacy in America are those which are economically deprived.' He, too, made the connection between Israel and American Jewry explicit with his contention that 'There is a symmetry between the hostility expressed toward the legitimacy of Israel as a Jewish state and the hostility expressed toward the legitimacy of the American-Jewish community as a distinct ethnic group.'[4] For Raab and others, anti-Zionism on the part of the political left could not be fully understood without an accompanying awareness of the left's attitudes about American Jews.

Since 1967, a leftist paradigm of identity politics has developed that uses a particular understanding of American race relations as a universal framework for understanding intergroup strife in general. Slogans such as 'From Ferguson to Palestine' suggest that the killing of an American Black man in Ferguson by a white police officer, an act which symbolized the high number of deaths of Black men at the hands of the police, was a model for explicating the Israeli-Palestinian conflict. Some even hinted at Israeli culpability for this quintessentially American assault.[5] Israelis can then be typecast solely as white and racist, Palestinians can be characterized as oppressed people of color, and a rigid binary of good and evil can be employed to explain the Israeli-Palestinian conflict. Any examples of Israeli suffering or vulnerability that challenge this model can therefore be ignored, rationalized, or attacked to remain consistent with this binary worldview.

In other words, Israel can be blamed for the Hamas attack. As a statement originally signed by 34 student groups at Harvard unequivocally announced, 'We, the undersigned student organizations, hold the Israeli regime entirely responsible for all unfolding violence.'[6] Even when facing violent attack, Israel is still portrayed as an oppressor.

Examples of the hostile attitudes of some on the left toward Israel after October 7 were easy to find. For instance, Russell Rickford, a history professor at Cornell, lauded the actions of Hamas at a political rally. Rickford framed Hamas attacks as a challenge to 'the monopoly of violence,' which he opined was held solely by Israel in the context of the conflict. He admitted that Hamas infiltrators had carried out 'horrific acts' that should be abhorred by those who condemn violence, yet he countered that the instances of murder, torture, and rape provided Gazans with the ability 'to breathe for the first time in years.' Rickford further claimed about these acts of violence that 'It was exhilarating. It was energizing. And if [Palestinians and Gazans] weren't exhilarated by this challenge to the monopoly of violence, by this shifting of the balance of power, then they would not be human. I was exhilarated.'[7]

Others saw no reason to hide their contempt for Israelis, denying them any aspect of humanity. At the School of the Art Institute of Chicago, Mika Tosca, an associate professor of climate science, lashed out after Israel began its incursion into Gaza in response to the Hamas attacks.

Israelis are pigs. Savages. Very very bad people. Irredeemable excrement. After the past week, if your eyes aren't open to the crimes against humanity that Israel is committing and has committed for decades, and will continue to commit, then I suggest you open them. It's disgusting and grotesque. May they all rot in hell.[8]

To maintain this callous relationship to the massacre and to the realities of Israeli vulnerability, inconvenient truths, such as the sexual violence employed by Hamas terrorists in its assault against Israeli citizens, were either ignored or rationalized. For instance, an associate professor at the Department of Gender, Women and Sexuality Studies at the University of Minnesota, Sima Shakhsari, denied the realities of the brutal attacks on Israeli women in an interview with a review panel for an associate dean role in the university's diversity, equity, and inclusion (DEI) department. Shakhsari rejected the overwhelming evidence of sexual assault from October 7 and asserted that those who made such accusations were not only liars but that their untruths were evidence of racism.

We know the history of lynching, of black man, lynching, of indigenous man lynching Latinos in this country … because of accusations and they're kind of violating the innocence of white women, right? And I think that is also this force that is repeated in the context of Israel and Palestine, because Arab men have been demonized and have been marked as monstrous people who are rapists and for violence.[9]

The need to reject or deny Israeli suffering contradicts a central tenet of leftist advocacy for gender equality and women's rights: victims of sexual assault should be believed. To rationalize this inconsistency, Shakhsari used the allegation of racism to supersede the claims made by and about Israeli women. In other words, Israeli women were not considered to be part of the community of those who experience the structural oppression of women in general. In their very experience of sexual violence, which targeted them as women, they were excluded from the protection offered by the left and by feminist principles. The intersectional nature of their identity was not honored as such, with their Israeli nationality overshadowing their traumatic victimization as women.

However, the animosity was not only directed at Israel. Some of it was aimed specifically at American Jews. A student at Cornell University, one of the most prestigious in the United States, was arrested for allegedly posting online threats to Jews that included shooting male students with assault rifles, raping and mutilating female students, and decapitating Jewish babies. He also threatened to 'bring an assault rifle to campus and shoot all you pig jews.' His threats mirrored the actions that Hamas terrorists had already taken against Israelis, suggesting that American Jews were deserving of similar treatment.[10]

Expressions of pain and fear by American Jews were also attacked, devalued, and denied by some segments of the left because the related understanding of Jews and the Jewish experience in the United States is one of uniform whiteness and privilege, leaving no space for the authenticity of Jewish vulnerability. Thus, while actress Susan Sarandon did not actively threaten violence, she did react to the precipitous rise in American antisemitism after Israel's incursion into Gaza, by suggesting that American Jews somehow deserved the violent threats, rhetoric, and actions aimed at them. At a rally, Sarandon opined, 'There are a lot of people that are afraid of being Jewish at this time and are getting a taste of what it feels like to be a Muslim in this country, so often subjected to violence.' Her comments served to normalize collective punishment against American Jews by suggesting that they were fair targets for antisemitic violence and hatred.[11]

Sarandon's remarks went beyond attacking Jews as Israel supporters. They were aimed squarely at Jews in general, and more specifically at denying the truth of Jewish victimization. Her comments, and those of other leftists, suggest that hateful rhetoric employed by parts of the political left is more than an attack against Israel. It is also a reaction used to express resentment toward Jews, to deny the realities of antisemitism, and to dismiss the sense of vulnerability that many Jews feel in contemporary American society. Additionally, Sarandon's statements were a classic example of the assumption that Jews are protected by white privilege, even though FBI statistics demonstrate that Jews, who are estimated to compose 2.4% of the population in the United States, are subject to some 60% of religiously motivated attacks.[12]

The need to delegitimize Jewish anxieties about the current climate in the United States was also conspicuous in an op-ed in the student newspaper for Wellesley College, in which a student author condemned the 'post-9/11 hysteria over the public usage of Arabic and Islamic words and phrases,' such as 'glory to our martyrs,' 'from the river to the sea,' and 'intifada.' In particular, she criticized a previous letter to the editor from students who objected to the phrase 'glory to our martyrs' as insensitive and antisemitic in the context of the October 7 attack. To this, the author retorted only that she 'would invite these students to examine their Islamophobia and anti-Arab racism.'[13]

Rather than acknowledging the possibility that Jewish students were acting to defend themselves against antisemitism in the wake of the calculated murder of Israeli citizens, the author defaulted immediately to counter-accusing those Jewish students of racism. One wonders at the powers of rationalization that might be required of the author to maintain her views if she were to be exposed to the antisemitic ideology of Hamas that is amply demonstrated in their original 1988 covenant, or the implacable opposition to Jewish peoplehood in the revised 2017 edition. Would the recent discovery of a highlighted edition of Adolf Hitler's *Mein Kampf* in a Hamas stronghold that emphasized passages calling for the mass murder of Jews be persuasive to the author?[14] Or the extant video of a Hamas terrorist exalting over his success at murdering ten Jews (the word he used was 'Jews' rather than 'Zionists' or 'Israelis') on October 7?[15] Or would all this still be deemed subsidiary to her allegation of Jewish privilege?

One of the consequences of the inability of individuals and organizations on the left to recognize Israeli suffering is that some American Jews, many of them political liberals, are forced to acknowledge the support tendered by right-wing political actors, sometimes even those who espouse antisemitic conspiracy theories about Jews. U.S. Representative Elise Stefanik (R-NY) gained the appreciation of many American Jews when she pointed out the hypocrisy of the presidents of elite American universities who refused to condemn calls for the genocide of the Jews at a December congressional hearing. Yet Stefanik has also been accused of supporting replacement theory, the conspiratorial allegation that liberals, in particular liberal Jews, plan to flood the United States with non-white immigrants to shift the balance of power away from conservatives and the Republican Party and steal control of America from white Christians.[16]

The fact that right-wing politicians are often outspoken in their defense of Israel also solidifies the connection between conservatism and support for Israel in some quarters of the left, and it provides antisemites on the left with an opportunity to conflate Jews with reactionary political movements. In an open letter published by a group calling itself 'Faculty for Justice in Palestine,' faculty members at Princeton employed racism as the central category of their analysis of the conflict without acknowledging antisemitism or admitting any Hamas culpability for the attacks. 'We refuse to muzzle our criticism of the Israeli siege and genocidal assault on Gaza, of apartheid in the occupied West Bank, and of structural racism and discrimination inside the state of Israel,' the authors pronounced. 'We stand against white supremacy in the United States and against Jewish supremacy in the land of Palestine/Israel.'[17]

The use of the term 'Jewish supremacy,' which some on the left have adopted to label the far right in Israel, or even Zionism as a whole, creates cognitive connections to white supremacy, just as the use of the apartheid analogy serves to reduce the conflict into an example solely of racism. Once these connections are made, there can be no nuance in the discussion: Israel and its supporters, no matter the actual content of their political views, can only be understood as racist oppressors. The term 'Jewish supremacy' also has a disreputable history stemming from its use by the Nazi movement in Germany. To resuscitate the term in the context of the conflict between Israel and Palestinians is akin to labeling Israel a Nazi state, which is as offensive as it is inaccurate.[18]

The hostile reaction after October 7 by some elements of the left is not a new phenomenon, although the intensity of that animosity was perhaps unprecedented. This acrimony has been building in some segments of the left since the 1967 War. Central to this antagonism is the characterization of Israel as an oppressive, racist, and colonial state in which whiteness is implied even when not stated. However, the representation of Jews only as white and privileged is an essential contributing factor to contemporary antisemitism. What was evident after October 7 is that any challenge to this model is also a challenge to this particular leftist worldview altogether, because it introduces ambiguity and complexity to stark, simple – and often inaccurate – moral binaries. The pushback against any evidence contrary to these binaries leads to the denial, rationalization, or glorification of violence and terror toward Israel, and the refusal to acknowledge the justified fears of American Jews.

Notes

1 Joshua Zeitz, "Anti-Israel Progressives Are Handing Liberal Jews an Impossible Decision, Just Like in 1967," *Politico Magazine*, 23 October 2023 (https://www.politico.com/news/magazine/2023/10/23/anti-israel-left-jewish-politics-00122848).

2 Seymour Martin Lipset, "The Return of Anti-Semitism as a Political Force." *Israel, the Arabs and the Middle East*, eds. Irving Howe and Carl Gershman (New York: Bantam Books, 1972) 391, 396.

3 Arnold Forster and Benjamin R. Epstein, *The New Anti-Semitism* (New York: McGraw Hill, 1974) 7, 16, 324.

4 Earl Raab, "Is There a New Anti-Semitism?" *Commentary*, 57 (1), January 1974, 55.

5 Mersiha Gadzo, "How the US and Israel Exchange Tactics in Violence and Control," *Al-Jazeera*, 12 June 2023 (https://www.aljazeera.com/news/2020/6/12/how-the-us-and-israel-exchange-tactics-in-violence-and-control).

6 J. Sellers Hill and Nia Orakwue, "Harvard Student Groups Face Intense Backlash for Statement Calling Israel 'Entirely Responsible' for Hamas Attack," *Harvard Crimson*, 10 October 2023 (https://www.thecrimson.com/article/2023/10/10/psc-statement-backlash/).

7 Sofia Rubinson, "Cornell Professor "Exhilarated" by Hamas's Attack Defends Remark," *Cornell Daily Sun*, 18 October 2023 (https://cornellsun.com/2023/10/16/cornell-professor-exhilarated-by-hamass-attack-defends-remark/).

8 Rebecca Rosenberg, "Chicago Professor Apologizes for Calling Israelis 'Pigs' and 'Savages'," *Fox 32 Chicago*, 20 October 2023 (https://www.fox32chicago.com/news/chicago-professor-calls-israelis-pigs-and-savages).

9 Michael Horovitz, "US Professor Who Denies Oct. 7 Rape Cases Up for Top Role at Campus Diversity Office," *Times of Israel*, 23 December 2023 (https://www.timesofisrael.com/us-professor-who-denies-oct-7-rape-cases-up-for-top-role-at-campus-diversity-office/).

10 U.S. Attorney's Office, Northern District of New York, "Press Release: Cornell Student Arrested for Making Online Threats to Jewish Students on Campus," 31 October 2023 (https://www.justice.gov/usao-ndny/pr/cornell-student-arrested-making-online-threats-jewish-students-campus).

11 Times of Israel Staff, "Susan Sarandon Apologizes for Saying US Jews 'Getting Taste' of Muslim Experience," *Times of Israel*, 2 December 2023 (https://www.timesofisrael.com/susan-sarandon-apologizes-for-saying-us-jews-getting-taste-of-muslim-experience/).

12 Hannah Rabinowitz, "FBI Director: Antisemitism Reaching 'Historic Level' in US," *CNN*, 31 October, 2023 (https://www.cnn.com/2023/10/31/politics/fbi-director-antisemitism-wray/index.html).

13 Maimoonah Shafqat, "Arabs and Muslims Will Speak For Ourselves," *Wellesley News*, 29 November 2023 (https://thewellesleynews.com/2023/11/29/arabs-and-muslims-will-speak-for-ourselves/).

14 Stuart Winer, "Herzog: Arabic Copy of 'Mein Kampf' Found on Hamas Terrorist Shows What War Is About," *Times of Israel*, 12 November 2023 (https://www.timesofisrael.com/herzog-arabic-copy-of-mein-kampf-found-on-hamas-terrorist-shows-what-war-is-about/).

15 Times of Israel Staff, "IDF Publishes Audio of Hamas Terrorist Calling Family to Brag about Killing Jews," *Times of Israel*, 25 October 2023 (https://www.timesofisrael.com/idf-publishes-audio-of-hamas-terrorist-calling-family-to-brag-of-killing-jews/).

16 Ron Kampeas, "'Is That Really Her?': Liberal Jews Split on Stefanik after Antisemitism Hearings," *Times of Israel*, 12 December 2023 (https://www.timesofisrael.com/is-that-really-her-liberal-jews-split-on-stefanik-after-antisemitism-hearings/).

17 Faculty for Justice in Palestine, "An Open Letter from Faculty for Justice in Palestine," *Daily Princetonian*, 29 November 2023 (https://www.dailyprincetonian.com/article/2023/11/princeton-opinion-opguest-faculty-for-justice-in-palestine-demand-free-speech-protection-divestment).

18 Gil Troy, "'Jewish Supremacy': A Nazi Slur Goes Woke," *Newsweek*, 25 June 2021 (https://www.newsweek.com/jewish-supremacy-nazi-slur-goes-woke-opinion-1603865).

5 A History of Feminist Antisemitism

Kara Jesella

It Wasn't Always Like This

The luckiest thing that ever happened in my academic life was having my rabbi teach my first Women's Studies course and Angela Davis teach my second.[1] At Vassar in the multiculti-and-identity-obsessed 1990s, I learned from this rabbi about intersectionality, black feminism, and that if I didn't understand the Spanish in the now-canonical anthology *This Bridge Called My Back: Writings by Radical Women of Color*, I had to find someone who did to translate it for me.[2] I also learned that I could be a Jewish feminist, parsing my own complicated personal and communal history for theoretical insights, like my favorite writer, Adrienne Rich.

In the first paper I wrote for the class—forgive me, I was 19—I compare my own experience to that of black Americans. During my 13 years as one of the only Jews in the Catholic schools I attended, the boy I sometimes thought was my boyfriend drew swastikas on my book covers. The boss at my summer job told me that Vassar would have 'a lot of JAPs there' (before explaining, in a series of epithets, just what a Jewish American Princess was). I didn't write about the panic of coming-of-age at a time—and in a city—where Operation Rescue picketed abortion clinics and screamed at 'baby-killers' every weekend. (A 1990 story in the Jewish feminist journal *Lilith* was headlined, 'The Anti-Choice Movement: Bad News for Jews.')[3] The year after I graduated—I had already fled to New York City—Barnett Slepian, a local Jewish doctor who performed abortions, was assassinated by a member of a Catholic anti-abortion group upon his return from shul.

Still, I concluded that blacks had it worse. 'I think you mute the terror of the swastika,' my rabbi remarked. She gave me an A-/A. Later, in Professor Davis's class, I learned that the term 'women of color' wasn't about melanin, it was an imaginative political formation. Those two classes informed everything I have done since: my undergraduate degree in Women's Studies, my years as a feminist journalist and book author, and the doctorate I received two years ago, when I finally completed my dissertation on feminist historiography.

DOI: 10.4324/9781003497424-5

May 2021 was a sad and scary month to be a Jewish feminist, as violence escalated in the Middle East and in New York City, where I still live. Friends from graduate school and the feminist internet posted anti-Zionist infographics on social media and a counterterrorism unit kept watch in front of my daughter's Jewish nursery school. The morning of my graduation, I awoke to a petition circulating on Twitter titled, 'Gender Studies Departments in Solidarity with Palestinian Feminist Collective.'[4] It informed me that Jews are colonizers not indigenous to Israel and rejected the International Holocaust Remembrance Alliance's definition of antisemitism. Two days later, I received an email from my department with news of an award, and another professing solidarity with the Palestinian people. It was hard to understand exactly what that meant—who doesn't want a better life for Palestinians?—but given the department's politics, I could guess.

But this was only a prelude of what was to come on October 7, 2023. Within hours of initial news reports about the atrocities committed by Hamas against the kibbutzim of southern Israel, feminist friends and colleagues began posting victorious images of Palestinian flags and paragliders to social media. Even more shocking than the reaction to the 1,200 men, women, and children who were murdered, and the 240 that were taken hostage, was the response to reports of torture and sexual cruelty that began to emerge. Many feminists were either reluctant or defiantly unwilling to show the slightest solidarity with Israeli women. Their priority lay instead with supporting calls to 'decolonize Palestine' by 'any means necessary.' Rape and sexual assault were scorned, denied, even excused as the legitimate or understandable acts of an oppressed people. There is no obvious reason for feminists to support Hamas, given the regressive ideas about female liberty and gender roles set out in the group's foundational covenant.[5] And yet, some feminists attended anti-Israel demonstrations at which eliminationist slogans were chanted, while others vandalized posters of the missing in the name of a free Palestine. Even the UN Women dragged its feet, taking eight weeks to condemn Hamas's sexual violence.

It wasn't always like this. In the years before the Second Intifada began in 2000, magazine and newspaper articles, books, and conference panels proliferated on Judaism and antisemitism.[6] Jewish feminists expressed their love for Israel, or at least an acknowledgment that the country needed to exist. Criticisms of Israeli policies often came from Jewish feminists themselves, who had no difficulty distinguishing Israeli citizens from the actions of their government. 'Jewish lesbian-feminists cannot help but feel critical toward the present Israeli government,' wrote Evelyn Torton Beck, a Women's Studies professor and child Holocaust survivor, in *Nice Jewish Girls: A Lesbian Anthology*, published in 1982.[7] 'In my writing and my activism, I support *both* the Palestinian and the Jewish national movements,' wrote Elly Bulkin in *Yours in Struggle: Three Feminist Perspectives on Anti-Semitism and Racism*, published in 1984.[8]

But changes in feminism's in-group formations and theorizations enabled the antisemitism and anti-Zionism that were latent at the advent of the
movement to become entrenched. The shift to identity-based feminism—
which includes the women-of-color feminism and queer theory now
predominant—has produced some exciting, inventive, moving, and sophis-
ticated feminist theory. But it has also contributed to an ideological climate
that scorns discussions of antisemitism and Israel and is profoundly inhos-
pitable to Jews.

From Sisterhood to Identity Politics

Jewish women have been an outsized force in feminism since the 1960s.
Florence Howe, who founded the Feminist Press and published lost feminist
works by black writers like Zora Neale Hurston, is known as the mother of
Women's Studies.[9] Roberta Salper, who established the first Women's Studies
Program in the country at San Diego State University in 1970, is also Jewish.[10] Many Jewish feminists were writers and organizers: Tillie Olsen, author
of *Silences*; Hélène Cixous, author of 'The Laugh of the Medusa'; 8 of the
12 members of the original Boston Women's Health Book Collective, which
published *Our Bodies, Ourselves*; the founder and several members of the
Jane Collective, which helped women obtain abortions when they were still
illegal.[11] Gerda Lerner, a Holocaust survivor, founded the first graduate program in Women's History and edited the acclaimed volume *Black Women in
White America*.[12] Shulamith Firestone, who was raised in an Orthodox home,
wrote *The Dialectic of Sex: The Case for Feminist Revolution*.[13]

In 1963, Jewish labor-journalist-turned-women's-magazine-writer Betty
Friedan kicked off feminism's second wave with *The Feminine Mystique*, in
which she wrote about the unfulfilling life of a housewife.[14] Younger 'radical feminists,' meanwhile, began dissecting sexuality and family life in their
consciousness-raising sessions. In 1970, Robin Morgan (also Jewish) wrote:

> Women's liberation is the first radical movement to base its politics—
> in fact, create its politics—out of concrete personal experiences. We've
> learned that those experiences are *not* our private hang-ups. They are
> shared by every woman, and are therefore political.[15]

But the title of Morgan's anthology *Sisterhood is Powerful* evokes an over-
reach that still haunts feminism today. Many Jewish feminists were socialists and staunch anti-racists—expatriates from the New Left and Civil Rights
movements, who had taken Black Power's injunction to 'organize your own'
seriously.[16] But their attempts to include women of color in their magazines
and conferences were, according to black feminist Toni Cade Bambara, 'invi-
tations to coalesce on their terms.'[17]

Most young women had been inspired by the protests against the Miss America Pageant they saw on television or by the manifestos against housework they read in *Ms.*[18] They hadn't studied Marx and Fanon, didn't know about forced sterilization, and weren't worried about affording food for their children. They simply wanted to fulfill feminism's first promise, which was to improve their own lives. There was plenty to do: it wasn't until the 1970s that unmarried women of any race or class could access the birth-control pill, terminate an unwanted pregnancy, obtain a credit card in their own name, or not get fired for being pregnant.

In the 1970s and 1980s, black, Chicana, Native American, Arab, and Asian women joined together to create a political bloc they called Third World Women, and later, Women of Color. Their texts insisted that oppression was not simply a product of gender but also of class, race, and sexual orientation. The Combahee River Collective Statement, which introduced 'identity politics' in 1977, says, 'If Black women were free, it would mean that everyone else would have to be free since our freedom would necessitate the destruction of all the systems of oppression.'[19] The black woman was a messianic figure, and she would bring liberation to the world.

Jewish feminists also insisted that they weren't like other white women, but they were not part of this burgeoning force. In *Feminist Theory: From Margin to Center*, published in 1984, black feminist bell hooks writes, 'Much feminist theory emerges from privileged women who live at the center.'[20] She was talking about white women in general, and Friedan in particular, whose most famous work hooks described as 'a case study of narcissism.'[21] The most visionary feminist theory, she wrote, will emerge from 'individuals who have knowledge of both margin and center.'[22] Growing up, Friedan was an infamously hook-nosed intellectual in Peoria, Illinois, rejected by peers because she was Jewish, yet excelling at graduate-level academics at a time when many universities refused to hire Jews.[23] But Jews were not considered marginal; feminist theory was to be written by—or at the very least about—women of color.

The newest texts, like black feminist Audre Lorde's 1981 National Women's Studies Association speech, 'The Uses of Anger,' encouraged feminists to redirect anger at men toward one another, a practice *This Bridge* co-editor and Chicana feminist Cherríe Moraga described that same year as 'an act of love.'[24] This ethic of confrontation and 'accountability' suffused the lesbian publishing scene that produced the most important feminist theory of the 1980s. In another speech from 1981, titled 'Coalition Politics: Turning the Century,' black feminist Bernice Johnson Reagon described the importance of 'trying to team up with somebody who could possibly kill you … because that's the only way you can figure you can stay alive.'[25] This process, she said, caused her to feel 'as if I'm gonna keel over any minute and die.'[26] Working together and feeling bad while doing it was the goal. In 1982, Angela Davis told women to become 'militant' about racism.[27] It became heroic to be what white feminist Mab Segrest would later call a 'race traitor.'[28]

By this time, Jewish women had started to gain worldly power, and not simply over nannies and housecleaners. Although—and this was the problem—they still had power over nannies and housecleaners, who were often women of color. Feminist publishing experimented with how women could share power. The majority-Jewish editorial collective behind *Conditions* invited Combahee members Barbara Smith and Lorraine Bethel to guest-edit the 1979 Black Women's Issue.[29] Bethel opened a poem titled 'What Chou Mean *We*, White Girl? Or, the Cullud Lesbian Feminist Declaration of Independence (Dedicated to the Proposition That All Women Are Not Equal, i.e. Identical/ly Oppressed)' by writing, '*Preface: I bought a sweater at a yard sale from a white-skinned (as opposed to Anglo-Saxon) woman. When wearing it I am struck by the smell—it reeks of a soft, privileged life without stress, sweat, or struggle.*'[30] A little more than 30 years after the Holocaust, it was not hard to understand who was being accused of easy living. In 1981's 'The Possibility of Life Between Us: A Dialogue Between Black and Jewish Women,' black women likewise insisted that Jews had it good.[31]

It wasn't just women of color who decided that Jewish women were too domineering, too successful, too white, too obsessed with the Holocaust, and too interested in their newfound ethnic identity as a way of dominating the newly identity-conscious feminist scene.[32] New-Age feminists believed that Judaism had killed goddess worship, and white socialist professors equated Jews with capitalists. But Jewish women had once considered women of color to be their natural allies, and now that the feminist theories and alliances of women of color were the most influential, it was their antisemitism that Jewish feminists called out most often. Women of color resented this criticism and said that it was racist.[33]

In 1988—six years after the publication of *Nice Jewish Girls* and a year before Kimberlé Crenshaw introduced the concept of intersectionality— Evelyn Torton Beck complained that Jewish women were being left out of Women's Studies.[34] She blamed 'our initial conceptual framework which established (and quickly *fixed*) the interlocking factors of "sex, race, and class" as *the* basis for the oppression of women.'[35] The prevailing analytical framework of Women's Studies was incapable of acknowledging that conspiratorial suspicions about Jewish advantage and influence actually *contributed* to their oppression.

Another problem Jewish feminists encountered was growing anti-Israel sentiment, a legacy of New Left and Black Power doctrines that understood the young country as imperialist, despite Jews' historic ties to the region, and even racist, as though the country's conflict pit white Jews against brown Arabs, despite the many Jews of color living there.[36] At the United Nations' International Women's Year Conference in Mexico City in 1975, delegates— many of whom hailed from Arab and African countries and saw Israel as the United States' client and a prop for Western hegemony—passed a motion equating Zionism with racism.[37] At Copenhagen in 1980, the conference extended official recognition to the Palestine Liberation Organization's delegation, headed by famed hijacker Leila Khaled.[38] Israel's retaliatory invasion of Lebanon in 1982 only increased hostility to Israel on the Western Left, and the brutality of that war made it hard for some Jewish women to defend the country.

Meanwhile, interest in Arab and postcolonial feminism was growing. In a 1983 issue of *Women's Studies Quarterly*, Azizah al-Hibri castigated Western feminists opposed to clitoridectomy and the veil instead of occupation and demanded, 'What good is my clitoris if *I* am not around?'[39] In *Yours in Struggle*, Barbara Smith wrote, 'Often Black and other women of color feel a visceral identification with the Palestinians,' even though, 'like many Black women, I know very little about the lives of other Third World women.'[40] The fantasy of an alliance with Third World women was more compelling than the reality of the obstinate Jewish women who had published some (but not enough) books by women of color, whom she publicly rebuked.[41] 'I am anti-Semitic,' she declared in the same essay, but she also wrote approvingly of a new and more complex Jewish feminism that supported the existence of Israel while opposing its government.[42] Women of color and Jewish feminists, including Zionists, were fighting in public—but at least some nuance remained, and the two sides were still talking.

Bridges to the New Feminist Antisemitism

In 1990, Jewish feminists who wanted to remain part of an increasingly international, multicultural, and intersectional feminist scene launched the aspirationally named *Bridges: A Journal for Jewish Feminists and Our Friends*.[43] The magazine's contributors participated in feminist conversations about identity and coalition-building by publishing and reviewing work by women of color, Jews of color, and Israeli and Arab peace activists. Many articles elaborated a formerly latent but now overt new identity: the secular, anti-racist, Jewishly identified, quite-possibly-lesbian feminist who was conversant in women-of-color feminist theory and supported a two-state solution at a time when the Jewish establishment still did not.

But the magazine's relentless promotion of the Good Jew helped to further demonize the Bad.

A diversity trainer wrote about not wanting to be a typical Brooklyn Jew, saying, 'I thought being Jewish was tied to upwardly-mobile class climbing and what I judged to be hypocritical behavior'; another writer said that she used to read about African Americans 'to escape my Jewishness, which seemed distinctly uncool.'[44] The Bad Jews were constantly 'harping on' anti-semitism and Israel, complained Rabbi Sharon Kleinbaum, the future leader of the iconic gay and lesbian Congregation Beit Simchat Torah.[45]

Melanie Kaye/Kantrowitz encouraged Good Jews to weaponize their Judaism against 'mainstream' Jews as a feminist act, and to consider the possibility that their charges of antisemitism were 'spurious.'[46] Good Jews, she wrote, 'have proudly reclaimed a tradition of radical Jews' (one that had nearly vanished because so many socialist, anti-capitalist, anti-Zionist, internationalist members of the Jewish Labor Bund in Eastern Europe were exterminated in the Holocaust).[47] *Bridges* publicized texts by Jewish feminists instrumental in developing what a 1997 *New York Times* article called the 'new, very hot academic field' of whiteness studies—a discipline that often recasts Jews' participation in the Civil Rights movement as *actually* racist because it was paternalistic.[48]

Other changes in feminist politics were also occurring. In 1990, Judith Butler published *Gender Trouble*, which argued that there is no natural correlation between biological sex and gender expression.[49] 'It has become a positive embarrassment to talk about women,' Women's Studies professor Nancy K. Miller had said the year before.[50] Queer theory brought feminists into increasing contact with theorists like Michel Foucault, who questioned individual agency, and they lost interest in lesbian feminism's emphasis on difficult but potentially productive engagement with opposing views.

In *Underdogs: Social Deviance and Queer Theory*, queer scholar Heather Love wrote that queer theory's politics 'are split between the liberalism of the civil rights movement and a lumpen appetite for destruction.'[51] This new 'queer' identity destroyed identity categories themselves, and the idea that 'everyone knows' that queer is not the same as lesbian and gay, said Love, 'creates a desire to be "in the know."'[52] Like the cultural ephemera it often turns to as its intellectual objects, queer theory thrived on the transgressive frisson of the unexpected and the illegitimate. If you're hip, you know that biology has nothing to do with being a man or a woman. You also know that Israel needs to be destroyed.

This combative energy soon became evident in the feminist literature of the early 2000s. The collapse of Israeli-Palestinian peace talks at Camp David, and the ruthless campaign of Palestinian suicide terror that followed, had made many Jewish organizations move rightward.[53] In response, progressive Jews began doing anti-occupation work elsewhere. Meanwhile, 9/11, Israeli military operations in the West Bank, the Bush administration's wars in Afghanistan and Iraq, the Patriot Act, and the debate about Islamophobia all increased American interest in the Middle East. New activist models dispensed with the idea that Israeli Jews and Palestinian Arabs both had legitimate claims to the land.

In 2003, an essay by Esther Kaplan titled 'Globalize the Intifada' appeared in the influential anthology, *Wrestling With Zion*. Kaplan was a former member of the queer AIDS activist group ACT UP, who succeeded Kaye/Kantrowitz as director of Jews for Racial and Economic Justice. In her essay, she called Palestine 'the new cause célèbre' and observed that activists 'have replaced the language of "conflict" and "peace" with that of "occupation" and "justice."'[54] Many of these activists now directed their message at non-Jews as well as Jews, an approach Kaplan supported and encouraged:

> … the time has come when Israel must be totally isolated by world opinion and forced, simply forced, to concede.

> The road to that victory will be littered with e-mail postings that are a bit strident and flyers that are insensitive to Jewish history. It will be populated by activists who are young, brash and unknowledgeable, a handful of whom will carry placards that read 'Zionism = Nazism' in a crude attempt to open old Jewish wounds. Israel will become a punching bag for every good reason and maybe a couple of bad ones, too. And so what?[55]

Feminist Icons: From the Queer Palestinian Terrorist to the Trans Anti-Zionist

'And so what?' The notion that there are bad nationalisms (those allied with the United States) and good nationalisms (those that were going to destroy capitalism and imperialism) was already part of leftist thought.[56] In 2004, Roderick A. Ferguson—a professor of Women's, Gender, and Sexuality Studies at Yale, and a future president of the Boycott, Divestment, and Sanctions-supporting American Studies Association—published *Aberrations in Black: Toward a Queer of Color Critique*, in which he offered this queer-theory-inflected reiteration of one of black feminism's earliest tenets: 'Oppositional coalitions have to be grounded in nonnormative racial difference. … Ours is a moment in which the negation of normativity and nationalism is the condition for critical knowledge.'[57] In 2005, the ultra-hip, ultra-leftist academic journal *Social Text* published 'What's Queer About Queer Studies Now?,' an essay that showcased the movement's turn away from 'the domestic affairs of white homosexuals' and toward Ethnic Studies and women-of-color feminism.[58]

Feminism further embraced what Love had called queer theory's 'injunction to be deviant.'[59] Jasbir K. Puar's 2005 essay, 'Queer Times, Queer Assemblages,' celebrated the Palestinian female suicide bomber, whose 'dispersion of the boundaries of bodies forces a completely chaotic challenge to normative conventions of gender, sexuality, and race, disobeying normative conventions of "appropriate" bodily practices and the sanctity of the able body.'[60] These 'queer corporealities' undermine the liberal Western tradition because 'suicide bombers do not transcend or claim the rational or accept the demarcation of the irrational.'[61] They are the apotheosis of what queer had always tried to be: not so much about sexual identity but about 'resistant bodily practices' and deviance itself—this time, across international boundaries.[62]

The ideal feminist persona had shifted from the educated working woman to the young radical to the lesbian woman of color, and now, to the queer

Palestinian terrorist. Meanwhile, Puar and others—including queer activist Sarah Schulman—would denigrate Israel's 'admittedly stellar' treatment of gays and lesbians as 'pinkwashing,' a means of distracting the world from its treatment of Palestinians.[63] Feminism's ongoing antipathy toward truth in favor of exhilaratingly counterintuitive theory, and a new set of desired effects and conclusions, had reached its apogee in attitudes toward Israel.

In her 2012 book, *Israel/Palestine and the Queer International*, Schulman argued that feminist activists don't need to be experts on the history or the politics of the Arab-Israeli conflict; they could rely instead on the arguments of those she called 'credibles.'[64] So, does Angela Davis, who published the 2016 anti-Zionist tract *Freedom is a Constant Struggle: Ferguson, Palestine, and the Foundations of a Movement*, qualify as credible?[65] That book was blurbed by Alice Walker—the Pulitzer-Prize-winning black feminist who unapologetically promotes the beliefs of David Icke, a Holocaust denier who claims the world is run by a secret cabal of Jewish alien lizards.[66] In her autobiography, Davis recalls how she delighted in Malcolm X's visit to her college, where he lambasted the white students there (many of whom were Jewish) for enslaving his people.[67] Another work is blurbed by Cynthia McKinney, who recently promoted an unambiguously antisemitic event on Twitter headlined by white supremacist David Duke.[68]

Schulman, for her part, doesn't like any Jews who aren't just like her. She describes a religious woman who wants to help her wash her hands 'in that awful Jewish way I remember from my childhood, so invasive you just can't breathe.'[69] When an Israeli 'warmly' invites her to join Jewish Voice for Peace, she 'immediately experienced that old recoil. I couldn't imagine joining a Jewish organization.'[70] Angry at her homophobic, Israel-loving biological family, Schulman acts out queer theory's celebration of chosen family, imagining a cruel 'queer international' in which a sense of belonging is solidified through partying, politics, and Israel-hatred.

Schulman is a seasoned activist—she was a leading member of the Lesbian Avengers—with a habit of parroting false history. She describes the diaspora as 'natural' and trains the novelistic skills that garnered her a Guggenheim on characterizing Judaism, the Jewish people, and Israel in exhaustively obscene ways.[71] Meanwhile, she fairly swoons when she gets a text that says 'we miss you' from some 'funny, warm, savvy, sexy, and totally accessible' new Palestinian friends.[72] They take photos together; they smoke pot; they chat about the ... what?—transfer? extermination?—of millions of Israeli Jews. 'We don't want peace,' they tell her.[73] What will happen to Israelis if her new political project succeeds? 'Israel exists,' she says airily.[74]

Schulman worships at the altar of Judith Butler, her number one credible besides her new Palestinian friends. Butler's 2003 essay, 'The Charge of Anti-Semitism: Jews, Israel, and the Risks of Public Critique,' is a theoretical rejoinder to former Harvard president Lawrence Summers's statement that 'profoundly anti-Israeli views are increasingly finding support in progressive intellectual communities. Serious and thoughtful people are advocating and taking actions that are anti-Semitic in their effect if not their intent.'[75] Butler's argument relies on the claim that Summers conflates Jews and Israel and assumes that the effects of antisemitism presuppose intentional antisemitism—which Summers neither said nor implied.[76]

In the years since, Butler and other Gender Studies luminaries have extended their anti-Zionist arguments. Butler, who claims that there is no essence to gender, believes that Jews do have an essence, and that it is diasporic.[77] Davis draws parallels between racist police violence in America and the occupation.[78] Puar says that Israel harvests Palestinian organs.[79] For Dean Spade, in his 2009 book, *Normal Life: Administrative Violence, Critical Trans Politics, and the Limits of Law*, trans politics are connected to Islamophobia because the United States' war on terror amplified 'security culture,' increasing surveillance policies that disproportionately disadvantage both Arabs and gender outlaws.[80] For example, a person whose gender expression does not match their sex may experience job discrimination, turn to illegal work, and end up in prison. This feminist anti-Zionism sees the existence of state-sanctioned gender categories as a violence that must be undone, even as it supports physical violence by non-state actors against Israelis. It is against liberalism and against rights, because rights, which are granted by the state, serve to prop up state power. The ideal feminist persona has morphed again: from queer Palestinian terrorist to trans anti-Zionist activist.

In the constitution of the National Women's Studies Association, passed in 1982, the group declared—over the objections of Jewish women and contrary to the term's definition—that it opposed antisemitism 'as directed against both Arabs and Jews.'[81] In 2015, the organization passed a BDS resolution.[82] In 2017, Linda Sarsour, a Women's March founder, announced that Zionists could not be feminists (and her co-chair, Tamika Mallory, defended the notoriously antisemitic Nation of Islam leader Louis Farrakhan).[83] That same year, Puar's book *The Right to Maim: Debility, Capacity, Disability* argued that Israel maims Palestinians on purpose and was rewarded with a major NWSA book prize.[84] In 2022, after most major Gender Studies departments signed the pledge in solidarity with Palestinians, Cary Nelson, author of 2019's *Israel Denial: Anti-Zionism, Anti-Semitism, and the Faculty Campaign Against the Jewish State*, called it 'a watershed moment' when 'academic programs for the first time officially represented themselves as vehicles of anti-Zionism.'[85]

Texts from the 1970s and 1980s still dominate feminist discourse—and inspire movements like Black Lives Matter—but *Nice Jewish Girls* and *Yours in Struggle* have been out of print for years.[86] There is now a cottage industry of white-women-are-bad books, like 2021's *The Trouble with White Women: A Counterhistory of Feminism*, in which Rutgers Women's, Gender, and Sexuality Studies professor Kyla Schuller writes that Betty Friedan (who, she points out, was born 'Betty Goldstein') 'advocated a form of biopolitics'—that is, optimizing the lives of white women at the expense of poor women and women

of color.[87] The white woman—that pariah of feminism, who, in her most ar-
chetypical form, looks, sounds, and quite obviously *is* Jewish—has become
worse than the patriarchy. She is a Nazi. A eugenicist. And like Israel itself, in
the works of these new feminist anti-Zionists, she wants women of color dead.

The Feminist-izing of Anti-Zionism

A version of this story ends back where it began: Women's Studies, born of
different strands of feminism, expelled women, thereby allowing the movement to return to its leftist roots. But feminism has also provided the Left with
new tools to rationalize its anti-Zionism. A 1990 book called *Jewish Women's
Call for Peace: A Handbook for Jewish Women on the Israeli/Palestinian
Conflict* suggests that Palestinian women are giving women hope that they
will 'succeed in destroying the patriarchal system.'[88]

In America, too, queer and/or black women are cast as resistors to the patriarchal United States, Israel, and male-dominated Jewish organizations.[89] In
Dean Spade's 2015 documentary, *Pinkwashing Exposed*, a Jewish Voice for
Peace activist employs the feminist vocabulary of rape to describe the Seattle
city council allowing an Israeli LGBTQ+ group to give a presentation—a
situation in which 'unsuspecting, uninformed folks with really good inten-
tions are brought into this against their will and consent.'[90] Meanwhile, actual
violence against gays and lesbians in Palestinian society—including abuse,
ostracism, and murder—is blamed on Israel's restrictions on mobility, which
prevents Palestinian queers from organizing.[91]

And feminism has given the Left the concept of intersectionality—a theoretical model designed to identify difference, but which now works to cover
it up. Today, it strives to wage social justice struggles by analogizing to the
point of false equivalence. This feminism, writes Angela Davis in *Freedom*,
urges us 'to think about things together that appear to be separate, and to dis-
aggregate things that appear to naturally belong together.'[92] White Western
women who try to join women in the Global South fighting for reproductive
rights or against rape and abuse are now imperialists guilty of assuming a false
sameness. But Ferguson, Missouri, *is* Palestine. Says Davis, 'I often like to
talk about feminism not as something that adheres to bodies, not as something
grounded in gendered bodies, but as an approach.'[93] This kind of feminism is
not necessarily by, about, or even sympathetic to women. It favors what feminist postcolonial theorist Gayatri Chakravorty Spivak calls 'strategic essential-
ism,' or the tactical deployment of identity while maintaining suspicion about
identity categories.[94] It promotes the suppression of speech over dialogue with
its support of BDS. It flourishes in Cultural Studies, American Studies, and
other 'Studies' fields with a myopic approach to intellectual topics.

'No U.S. Aid for Genocide!' a Gender Studies professor I had once
been on a panel with posted a week after the October 7th massacre. 'Stand
on the right side of history.' It is clear that feminists no longer understand

history—certainly not the history of Israel or Jews or the Zionist feminists who spent years working for peace—nor do they care. Today's feminist theory is art pretending to be history, brilliantly referencing and riffing on older feminisms, and offering blueprints for a new and supposedly better world—a world in which, as in many leftist iterations past, the destruction of Israel is a foregone conclusion.

Notes

1 A version of this essay was published in *Quillette* on 15 December 2023. Available at: https://quillette.com/2023/12/15/a-history-of-feminist-antisemitism/ (Accessed: 31 December 2023). Thank you to my editor, Jamie Palmer.

2 Moraga, C. and Anzaldúa, G. (eds.) ([1981] 1983) *This Bridge Called My Back: Writings by Radical Women of Color*. New York: Kitchen Table: Women of Color Press.

3 Weidman Schneider, S. (1990) 'The Anti-Choice Movement: Bad News for Jews', in *Lilith*. 12 June 1990. Available at: https://lilith.org/articles/the-anti-choice-movement-bad-news-for-jews/ (Accessed: 29 December 2023).

4 Palestinian Feminist Collective (2021) *Gender Studies Departments in Solidarity with Palestinian Feminist Collective*. Available at: http://genderstudiespalestine-solidarity.weebly.com/ (Accessed: 29 December 2023).

5 Islamic Resistance Movement (1988) *Hamas Covenant 1988*. Yale Law School Lillian Goldman Law Library The Avalon Project Documents in Law, History and Diplomacy. Available at: https://avalon.law.yale.edu/20th_century/hamas.asp (Accessed: 29 December 2023).

6 Antler, J. (2018) *Jewish Radical Feminism: Voices from the Women's Liberation Movement*. New York: New York University Press.

7 Beck, E. T. (1982) 'Next Year in Jerusalem?', in Beck, E. T. (ed.) *Nice Jewish Girls: A Lesbian Anthology*. Watertown: Persephone Press, Inc. p. 194.

8 Bulkin, E. ([1984] 1988) 'Hard Ground: Jewish Identity, Racism, and Anti-Semitism', in Bulkin, E., Pratt, M. B., and Smith, B. (eds.) *Yours in Struggle: Three Feminist Perspectives on Anti-Semitism and Racism*. Ithaca: Firebrand Press, p. 155.

9 Wertheim, B. (2020) 'Florence Howe, "Mother of Women's Studies," Dies at 91', in *New York Times*. 13 September 2020. Available at: https://www.nytimes.com/2020/09/13/us/florence-howe-dead.html (Accessed: 29 December 2023).

10 Salper, R. (2014) *Domestic Subversive: A Feminist's Take on the Left 1960-1976*. Tucson: Anaphora Literary Press.

11 Olsen, T. ([1978] 2003) *Silences*. New York: The Feminist Press at the City University of New York; Cixous, H. (1976) 'The Laugh of the Medusa.' Translated from the French by Cohen, K. and Cohen, P. *Signs*, 1(4), pp. 875–893. Available at: http://www.jstor.org/stable/3173239 (Accessed: 29 December 2023); Antler, *supra* note vi, at p. 158; and Ghert-Zand, R. (2022) 'When a Secret Group of Chicago Women Defied the Law to Provide 11,000 Safe Abortions', in *Times of Israel*. 7 June 2022. Available at: https://www.timesofisrael.com/when-a-secret-group-of-chicago-women-defied-the-law-to-provide-11000-safe-abortions/ (Accessed: 29 December 2023).

12 Lerner, G. (ed.) ([1972] 1992) *Black Women in White America: A Documentary History*. New York: Vintage Books.

13 Firestone, S. (1970) *The Dialectic of Sex: The Case for Feminist Revolution*. New York: William Morrow.

14 Friedan, B. ([1963] 1997) *The Feminine Mystique*. New York: W.W. Norton & Company.

15 Morgan, R. (1970) 'Introduction: The Women's Revolution', in Morgan, R. (ed.) *Sisterhood Is Powerful: An Anthology of Writings from The Women's Liberation Movement*. New York: Random House, pp. xvii–xviii.

16 Roth, B. ([2004] 2007) *Separate Roads to Feminism: Black, Chicana, and White Feminist Movements in America's Second Wave*. New York: Cambridge University Press and Antler, *supra* note vi.

17 Cade Bambara, T. ([1981] 1983). 'Foreword', in Moraga, C. and Anzaldúa, G. (eds.), *supra* note ii, at p. vi.

18 Freeman, J. (1975) *The Politics of Women's Liberation*. New York: David McKay Company, Inc., p. 85.

19 Combahee River Collective (1977) ([1981] 1983) 'A Black Feminist Statement', in Moraga, C. and Anzaldúa, G. (eds.), *supra* note ii, at pp. 212, 215.

20 hooks, b. (1984) *Feminist Theory: From Margin to Center*. Boston: South End Press, p. x.

21 Ibid. p. 3.

22 Ibid. p. ix.

23 Schuller, K. (2021) *The Trouble with White Women: A Counterhistory of Feminism*. New York: Bold Type Books, pp. 152–153.

24 Lorde, A. (1981) 'The Uses of Anger', in *Women's Studies Quarterly*, 9(3), pp. 7–10. Available at: https://www.jstor.org/stable/40003905 (Accessed: 29 December 2023) and Moraga, C. ([1981] 1983) 'And When You Leave, Take Your Pictures with You: Racism in the Women's Movement', in Moraga, C. and Anzaldúa, G. (eds.), *supra* note ii, at p. 62.

25 Reagon, B. J. (1981) 'Coalition Politics: Turning the Century', in Smith, B. (ed.) (1983) *Home Girls: A Black Feminist Anthology*. New York: Kitchen Table: Women of Color Press, pp. 356–357.

26 Ibid. p. 356.

27 Davis, A. (1982) 'Women, Race and Class: An Activist Perspective', in *Women's Studies Quarterly*, 10(4), p. 8. Available at: https://www.jstor.org/stable/40004176 (Accessed: 29 December 2023).

28 Segrest, M. ([1994] 2019) *Memoir of a Race Traitor: Fighting Racism in the American South*. New York: The New Press.

29 Smith, B. (1983) 'Introduction', in Smith, B. (ed.), *supra* note xxv, at pp. xlviii–l; Enszer, J. R. (2015) '"Fighting to Create and Maintain Our Own Black Women's Culture": *Conditions* Magazine, 1977–1990', in *American Periodicals: A Journal of History and Criticism*, 25(2), pp. 160–176. Available at: https://doi.org/10.1353/amp.2015.0025 (Accessed: 29 December 2023).

30 Bethel, L. (1979) 'What Chou Mean *We*, White Girl? Or, the Cullud Lesbian Feminist Declaration of Independence (Dedicated to the Proposition That All Women Are Not Equal, i.e. Identical/ly Oppressed)', in *Conditions: Five/The Black Women's Issue*, p. 86. Available at: https://www.lesbianpoetryarchive.org/sites/default/files/Conditions%205.pdf (Accessed: 30 December 2023).

31 Smith, B., et al. (1981) '"The Possibility of Life between Us': A Dialogue between Black and Jewish Women', in *Conditions: Seven*, pp. 25–46. Available at: https://www.lesbianpoetryarchive.org/sites/default/files/ConditionsSevenB&W.pdf (Accessed: 30 December 2023).

32 Beck, *supra* note vii; Pogrebin, L. C. (1982) 'Anti-Semitism in the Women's Movement', in *Ms.*, June 1982. Available at: https://jwa.org/media/anti-semitism-in-womens-movement-by-letty-cottin-pogrebin (Accessed: 30 December 2023); Bulkin, Pratt, and Smith (eds.), *supra* note viii, and Antler, *supra* note vi.

33 Smith, *supra* note xxv, at p. xliv; and Smith, B. ([1984] 1988) 'Between a Rock and a Hard Place: Relationships between Black and Jewish Women', in Bulkin, Pratt, and Smith (eds.), *supra* note viii, at pp. 7–78.

34 Crenshaw, K. (1989) 'Demarginalizing the Intersection of Race and Sex: A Black Feminist Critique of Antidiscrimination Doctrine, Feminist Theory and Antiracist Politics', in *University of Chicago Legal Forum*, 1989(1), pp. 139–167. Available at: http://chicagounbound.uchicago.edu/uclf/vol1989/iss1/8 (Accessed: 30 December 2023) and Beck, E. T. (1988) 'The Politics of Jewish Invisibility', in *NWSA Journal*, 1(1), pp. 93–102. Available at: https://www.jstor.org/stable/4315868 (Accessed: 30 December 2023).

35 Ibid. p. 101.

36 Beck, *supra* note vii; Pogrebin, *supra* note xxxii; Beck *supra* note xxxiv; Norwood, S. H. (2013) *Antisemitism and the American Far Left*. New York: Cambridge University Press; Dollinger, M. (2018) *Black Power, Jewish Politics: Reinventing the Alliance in the 1960s*. Waltham: Brandeis University Press; and Antler, *supra* note vi.

37 Olcott, J. (2017) *International Women's Year: The Greatest Consciousness-Raising Event in History*. New York: Oxford University Press.

38 Schreiber, R. (1981) 'Copenhagen: One Year Later', in *Lilith*. 22 June 1981. Available at: https://lilith.org/articles/copenhagen-one-year-later/ (Accessed: 30 December 2023).

39 al-Hibri, A. (1983) 'Unveiling the Hidden Face of Racism: The Plight of Arab American Women', in *Women's Studies Quarterly*, 11(3), pp. 10–11. Available at: https://www.jstor.org/stable/40004220 (Accessed: 30 December 2023).

40 Smith ([1984] 1988) 'Between a Rock and a Hard Place: Relationships between Black and Jewish Women', in Bulkin, Pratt, and Smith (eds.), *supra* note viii, at pp. 83, 70.

41 Enszer, J. R. (2013) *The Whole Naked Truth of Our Lives: Lesbian Feminist Print Culture from 1969 through 1989*. Unpublished: University of Maryland, College Park. PhD, pp. 145–225 and Gilley, J. (2016) 'Feminist Publishing/Publishing Feminism: Experimentation in Second-Wave Book Publishing', in Harker, J. and Konchar Farr, C. (eds.) *This Book Is an Action: Feminist Print Culture and Activist Aesthetics*. Chicago: University of Illinois Press, pp. 35–42.

42 Smith ([1984] 1988) 'Between a Rock and a Hard Place: Relationships between Black and Jewish Women', in Bulkin, Pratt, and Smith (eds.), *supra* note viii, at pp. 69, 82.

43 *Bridges* (1990–2011). Bridges Association. Available at: https://www.jstor.org/journal/bridges#:~:text=Bridges%20is%20a%20showcase%20for,interviews%2C%20diaries%2C%20and%20letters (Accessed: 3 January 2024).

44 Lippin, T. M. (1990) 'Responses: On Faith Rogow's *The Rise of Jewish Lesbian-Feminism*', in *Bridges* 1(2), p. 8. Available at: https://www.jstor.org/stable/40358466 (Accessed: 30 December 2023) and Stein, A. (2000) 'Anthologizing Ambivalences. Review of *Insider/Outsider: American Jews and Multiculturalism*, edited by Biale, D., Galchinsky, M. and Heschel, S.', in *Bridges* 8(1/2), p. 129 Available at: https://www.jstor.org/stable/40358562 (Accessed: 30 December 2023).

45 Kleinbaum, S. (1991) 'Enriching Our Cultural Life. Review of *Partisans of Vilna: The Songs of World War II Jewish Resistance* by Kempner, A. et al.', in *Bridges* 2(1), p. 117. Available at: https://www.jstor.org/stable/40358698 (Accessed: 31 December 2023).

46 Kaye/Kantrowitz, M. (2007) *The Colors of Jews: Racial Politics and Radical Diasporism*. Bloomington: Indiana University Press, p. 110.

47 Ibid. p. 135.

48 Talbot, M. (1997) 'Getting Credit for Being White', in *New York Times Magazine*. 30 November 1997. Available at: https://www.nytimes.com/1997/11/30/magazine/getting-credit-for-being-white.html (Accessed: 30 December 2023) and Bulkin, E. ([1984] 1988) 'Hard Ground: Jewish Identity, Racism, and Anti-Semitism', in Bulkin, Pratt, and Smith (eds.) *supra* note viii, at p. 92.

49 Butler, J. ([1990] 2006) *Gender Trouble: Feminism and the Subversion of Identity*. New York: Routledge.

50 Miller, N. (1989) 'Criticizing Feminist Criticism', in Hirsch, M. and Keller E. F. (eds.) (1990) *Conflicts in Feminism*. New York: Routledge, p. 351.

51 Love, H. (2021) *Underdogs: Social Deviance and Queer Theory*. Chicago: The University of Chicago Press, pp. 77–78.

52 Ibid. p. 3.

53 Kaplan, E. (2003) '"Globalize the Intifada"', in Kushner, T. and Solomon, A. (eds.) *Wrestling with Zion: Progressive Jewish-American Responses to the Israeli-Palestinian Conflict*. New York: Grove Press, pp. 81–88.

54 Ibid. pp. 83, 86.

55 Ibid. pp. 87–88.

56 Higashida, C. (2011) *Black Internationalist Feminism: Women Writers of the Black Left, 1945–1995*. Chicago: University of Illinois Press.

57 Ferguson, R. A. (2004) *Aberrations in Black: Toward a Queer of Color Critique*. Minneapolis: University of Minnesota Press, pp. 137, 141.

58 Eng, D. L., Halberstam, J., and Muñoz, J. E. (eds.) (2005) "Introduction: What's Queer about Queer Studies Now?" *Social Text* 84–85 23(3–4), pp. 1–17, 12. Available at: https://read.dukeupress.edu/social-text/article/23/3-4%20(84-85)/1/32709/ Introduction (Accessed: 30 December 2023).

59 Love, *supra* note li, at p. 37.

60 Puar, J. K. (2005) 'Queer Times, Queer Assemblages', in *Social Text* 84–85 23(3–4), pp. 131, 121–139. Available at: https://doi.org/10.1215/01642472-23-3-4_84-85-121 (Accessed: 30 December 2023).

61 Ibid. pp. 121, 130.

62 Ibid. pp. 131.

63 Puar, J. K. (2017) *The Right to Maim: Debility, Capacity, Disability*. Durham: Duke University Press, p. 96 and Schulman, S. (2011) 'Israel and "Pinkwashing"', in *New York Times*. 2011 November 22. Available at: https://www.nytimes.com/2011/11/23/opinion/pinkwashing-and-israels-use-of-gays-as-a-messaging-tool.html (Accessed: 30 December 2023).

64 Schulman, S. (2012) *Israel/Palestine and the Queer International*. Durham: Duke University Press, pp. 24, 36, etc.

65 Davis, A. Y. (2016) *Freedom Is a Constant Struggle: Ferguson, Palestine, and the Foundations of a Movement*. Chicago: Haymarket Books.

66 Alter, A. (2018) 'Alice Walker, Answering Backlash, Praises Anti-Semitic Author as "Brave"', in *New York Times*. 2018 December 21. Available at: https://www.nytimes.com/2018/12/21/arts/alice-walker-david-icke-times.html (Accessed: 30 December 2023).

67 Davis, A. ([1974] 1988) *Angela Davis: An Autobiography*. New York: International Publishers, pp. 117–127.

68 Davis, A. Y. (2003) *Are Prisons Obsolete?* New York: Seven Stories Press and McKinney, C. (2023) 'I Know Where I'll Be and What I'll Be Watching at 6:00 PM EASTERN Time Today! Can Black People and White People Work Together to Defeat Our Common Enemy?' *Twitter*. 11 September 2011. Available at https://twitter.com/cynthiamckinney/status/1701387020931604591 (Accessed: 30 December 2023).

69 Schulman, *supra* note lxiv, p. 98.

70 Ibid. p. 59.

71 Ibid. p. 12.

72 Ibid. pp. 140, 106.

73 Ibid. p. 148.

74 Ibid. p. 60.

75 Butler, J. (2003) 'The Charge of Anti-Semitism: Jews, Israel, and the Risks of Public Critique', in Kushner, T. and Solomon, A. (eds.) *Wrestling with Zion: Progressive Jewish-American Responses to the Israeli-Palestinian Conflict*. New York: Grove Press, p. 249.
76 Ibid. pp. 249–265.
77 Butler, J. (2012) *Parting Ways: Jewishness and the Critique of Zionism*. New York: Columbia University Press.
78 Davis, *supra* note lxv.
79 Wanderman, M. (2016) 'US professor: Israel assassinates, harvests organs', in *Israel National News*. 9 February 2016. Available at: https://www.israelnationalnews.com/news/207758 (Accessed 23 December 2023).
80 Spade, D. ([2009] 2015). *Normal Life: Administrative Violence, Critical Trans Politics, and the Limits of Law*. Durham: Duke University Press, p. 80.
81 Beck, *supra* note xxxiv, at p. 95.
82 National Women's Studies Association (2015) 'NWSA Statement Solidarity'. 19 January 2015. Available at: https://www.nwsa.org/news/483386/NWSA-Statement-Solidarity.htm (Accessed: 30 December 2023).
83 Meyerson, C. (2017) 'Can You Be a Zionist Feminist? Linda Sarsour Says No', in *The Nation*. 13 March 2017. Available at: https://www.thenation.com/article/archive/can-you-be-a-zionist-feminist-linda-sarsour-says-no/ (Accessed: 30 December 2023) and Mallory, T. D. (2017) 'Thank God This Man Is Still Alive and Doing Well. He Is Definitely the GOAT. Happy Birthday…', *Twitter*. 11 May 2017. Available at https://twitter.com/TamikaDMallory/status/862760808232517633 (Accessed: 30 December 2023).
84 Puar, *supra* note lxiii.
85 Nelson, C. (2022) 'The Anti-Israel Politicisation of the US Academy: The Next Phase is Happening at California and Illinois', in *Fathom Journal*. May 2022. Available at: https://fathomjournal.org/the-anti-israel-politicisation-of-the-us-academy-the-next-phase-is-happening-at-california-and-illinois/ (Accessed: 30 December 2023).
86 Taylor, K. (ed.) 2017 *How We Get Free: Black Feminism and the Combahee River Collective*. Chicago: Haymarket Books.
87 Schuller, *supra* note xxiii, at pp. 152, 163.
88 Espanioli, N. (1989) 'Women Go for Peace Conference', in Falbel, R., Klepfisz, I., and Nevel, D. (eds.) (1990) *Jewish Women's Call For Peace: A Handbook for Jewish Women on the Israeli/Palestinian Conflict*. Ithaca: Firebrand Books, p. 34.
89 Falbel, Klepfisz, and Nevel (eds.), *supra* note lxxxviii; Kaye/Kantrowitz, *supra* note xlvi, and Davis, *supra* note lxv, at p. 86.
90 Spade, D. (Director) (2015) *Pinkwashing Exposed: Seattle Fights Back*. [Film]. Available at: https://www.youtube.com/watch?v=AfpvrsZ-LtU (Accessed: 30 December 2023).
91 Puar, *supra* note lxiii, at p. 120.
92 Davis, *supra* note lxv, at p. 104.
93 Ibid. p. 27.
94 Spivak, G. C. (1984) 'Criticism, Feminism, and the Institution: An Interview with Gayatri Chakravorty Spivack', Interview with E. Grosz (1985) in *Thesis Eleven*, 10/11(1), pp. 175–187. Available at: https://doi.org/10.1177/072551368501000113 (Accessed: 30 December 2023).

6   The Return of the Progressive Atrocity

Susie Linfield[1]

In 1957, Albert Memmi addressed the question of the Left's relationship to terrorism in his book *The Colonizer and the Colonized*. Memmi was a Tunisian Jew who was equally committed to socialism, Zionism, and anti-colonialism. The Left tradition, he observed, 'condemns terrorism' as 'incomprehensible, shocking and politically absurd. For example, the deaths of children and persons outside the struggle.'[2]

But Memmi's suppositions were outdated even as he wrote. The history of the modern Left's romance with terrorism – not the 'old-fashioned' version aimed at czars or imperial officials, but the now-familiar kind directed against unarmed civilians – had already begun. It started with the Algerian War and gained momentum throughout the 1960s, 1970s, and beyond with the emergence of the Red Brigades, the Baader-Meinhof Gang, the Irish Republican Army, the Japanese Red Army, the Weathermen, and the panoply of organizations included in the Palestine Liberation Organization and, especially, its Rejectionist Front. The latter held pride of place: 'For the Sixth International, the Palestinian resistance is a banner, ... an inspiration for the revolt of the dispossessed, both in its ends and in its means,'[3] proclaimed Mohamed Sid-Ahmed, a prominent Egyptian leftwing intellectual and activist.

It was at this time that the oxymoronic and ethically repellent concept of what the late Middle East scholar and socialist Fred Halliday criticized as 'progressive atrocities' gained credence on the Left, particularly within the Palestinian movement and the groups that supported it. Of course, the Palestinian national project – like Zionism – has always contained a variety of ideologies ranging from peaceful coexistence to the elimination of the other. (The latter tendency is appallingly prevalent among many members of Benjamin Netanyahu's current government.) But it is no exaggeration to say that the Palestinian movement, even before the founding of Israel in 1948, has been defined by terror perhaps more than any other, and that terrorist groups have reigned supreme *within* the movement.

In the age of the 'progressive atrocity,' PLO attacks on Israelis, Jews, and civilians throughout the world were hailed as liberatory. A very partial list of such incidents would include the murder of the Israeli athletes at the 1972

DOI: 10.4324/9781003497424-6

Olympics (the games continued, nonetheless) and the Lod Airport massacre (death toll: 26, along with at least 80 injured) the same year; the Ma'alot massacres of 1974, in which 115 Israelis, mainly schoolchildren, were taken hostage (resulting deaths: 31); the 1982 attack on the Chez Jo Goldenberg kosher restaurant in Paris, considered, at the time, the worst incidence of anti-Semitism in France since the Holocaust (death toll: 6, with 22 injured); the Entebbe hijacking of 1976, in which Israeli and other Jewish passengers were separated from others and threatened with death (most were rescued by Israeli commandos); the 1978 Coastal Road massacre, in which a civilian bus was highjacked (death toll: 38, including 13 children; 71 wounded); and numerous airplane hijackings. Various international groups, especially Baader-Meinhof of Germany and the Japanese Red Army, sometimes assisted their Palestinian brothers 'in solidarity.' Not all leftists or Left organizations supported these actions, but to criticize them was a sign of 'bourgeois moralism,' as Ghassan Kanafani, a leader of the Popular Front for the Liberation of Palestine, put it.[4] (Kanafani, who was also a gifted writer, was assassinated after the Lod attack by the Mossad.)

Curiously, none of the groups utilizing terrorism achieved its aims, other than the Algerian National Liberation Front. (Well, sort of. The Algerians gained their independence, but the regime established by the NLF remains one of the most repressive on Earth. The NGO Freedom House ranks Algeria as 'not free,' its worst category.) The revolutions that did succeed – Chinese, Vietnamese, Cuban, Nicaraguan, and South African – weren't nonviolent, but they largely refrained from attacks on unarmed civilians. Indeed, Marxist movements had traditionally shunned terror against civilians on both moral and political grounds. Terror against civilians demoralizes ordinary people and almost always pushes them to the Right, often into the arms of authoritarian leaders; terrorism exalts the singular act as opposed to building a mass movement. André Malraux's 1928 novel *The Conquerors*, set during the failed Chinese Communist uprising of 1925, opens with a singular, dramatic act of terror; it is Garine, the book's hero and a Marxist, who opposes this. The dire state of the Palestinian movement today strongly suggests that there is an inverse relationship between the use of terror and the achievement of freedom.

In recent years, the Left's embrace of terror has ebbed; you won't find many defenders of Al-Qaeda, ISIS, the Taliban, or Boko Haram. The notable exception has been groups devoted to the destruction of Israel: Hamas, Islamic Jihad, and Hezbollah, which still garner enthusiasm and deluded admiration. One would have thought that an orgy of sadistic murder – Hamas's assault of October 7 – would have shaken these fellow travelers out of their perverse regard for jihadist terror and inspired a serious self-interrogation, both moral and political, of their obsessive hatred for Israel. As the past several weeks have illustrated, the exact opposite is the case.

The extraordinary nature of the pro-Palestinian demonstrations that have swept the capitals of the West – demonstrations that, crucially, *began before*

Israel dropped a single bomb on Gaza – has, perhaps, not been fully appreciated. Horrific massacres of unarmed civilians are, unfortunately, taking place right now: think of South Sudan, Congo, Ethiopia, Syria, and Darfur. Sadly – indeed, unforgivably – the so-called international community often, in fact usually, ignores them. But none inspires cries of esteem for the perpetrators and acclaim for their crimes. And nowhere are the victims – defenseless civilians, including children and their mothers – blamed for being murdered. That is what is happening now. The deadliest single day in the post-Holocaust history of the Jewish people has been greeted with joy and – let's be blunt – an entirely undisguised hatred of Jews.

Many of the sentiments that have been expressed – on social media, during street marches, and in the pages of various publications – reveal an astonishing distance from anything that might be considered rational political judgment and ordinary humanity. At the 'All Out for Palestine' rally in Times Square, held only one day after the massacre, elated chants of '700!' – the number of estimated Israeli deaths at the time – rang out, and demonstrators made throat-slitting gestures. A speaker at a Palestine Solidarity Campaign rally in Brighton, England, also held on October 8, described the attacks as 'beautiful and inspiring.'[5] The image of a hang-glider – just like the ones Hamas used! – with a Palestinian flag has gone viral on the web, posted by everyone from Black Lives Matter/Chicago to neo-Nazi groups, which gives intersectionality a whole new meaning.

It is likely that many of these groups – especially those composed of privileged students who promiscuously toss about words like 'genocide,' 'settler-colonialism,' and 'fascism' – have scant if any knowledge of Middle East politics or history and couldn't tell you the difference between the river and the sea. Many are signaling their 'anti-colonial' credentials, though I imagine that the usually stern Ayatollah Ali Khamenei in Tehran is smiling in amazed delight as he sees just *how many* protestors in the West echo his thoughts and subscribe to his oft-stated plan to destroy the 'Zionist entity,' even if they don't quite know that they're doing so.

But others, including presumably knowledgeable intellectuals, also quickly jumped in. In the *New Left Review*, Britain's leading Marxist journal, Tariq Al praised the terrorists for 'rising up against the colonizers' and implied, bizarrely, that the murders resulted from Palestinian frustration with Israel's enormous pro-democracy demonstrations.[6] In the *London Review of Books*, Amjad Iraqi noted the horrifying nature of the attacks but praised them for having 'shatter[ed] a psychological barrier,' though it might be argued that civilization depends on the maintenance of certain barriers.[7] In *Dissent*, a journal with which I have long been associated and that was formerly the home of Michael Walzer's liberal-left Zionism, history professor Gabriel Winant described Israel as a 'genocide machine' and argued that Israeli victims should not be grieved.[8] Joseph Massad, a tenured professor at Columbia University who teaches Middle Eastern studies, was unable to contain his enthusiasm:

The attacks were 'innovative,' 'astonishing,' a 'major achievement,' 'awesome,' 'incredible,' and 'a stunning victory'; he wondered with excitement 'if this is the start of the Palestinian War of Liberation.'[9] (Thousands have signed a petition demanding that Massad be fired; tempting though this is, I maintain my free speech principles, though these are the times that try them.) The inaptly named Students for Justice in Palestine, the most verbally bloodthirsty of student groups, declared 'Glory to Our Martyrs,' described the massacre as 'a historic win,' and demanded 'Do not let Western media call this terrorism. This is DECOLONIZATION.'[10] To equate such pro-Hamas groups and activists with being 'pro-Palestinian' should be a misnomer, just as it would be to call violent settlers in the West Bank 'pro-Israel.'

Yet the clear implication – often overtly expressed – of the demonstrators, the articles, the cascade of statements and open letters is that the October 7 attacks and the Palestinian national project *are* synonymous. If not, why do so many demonstrators lustily echo the Hamas program? (At my own university, much to my shame: 'We don't want no two states, we want all of it.')[11] I have seen many signs equating Zionism with genocide and fascism, but not one that says, 'Palestine Yes, Hamas No.' Even among those who would never actually align themselves with a terror group, there is cursory – and sometimes zero – condemnation of the killers, which is replaced by censure of Zionism as a presumably racist-imperialist project and by hasty pivots to the so-called 'root cause.'

Why the euphemistic language, as if the Left is too delicate to look atrocity in the face? At Columbia, 130 professors, prominent scholars among them, characterized the massacres as a 'military operation,'[12] which unfortunately echoes Vladimir Putin's description of his invasion of Ukraine as a 'special military operation.' (October 7 was also quite special.) In *The New York Review of Books*, some of our country's most esteemed writers, including Ta-Nehisi Coates and Richard Ford – who surely know the difference between language that clarifies and language that occludes – described the murderous rampage in an odd way: 'On Saturday, after sixteen years of siege, Hamas militants broke out of Gaza.'[13]

Why the cowardly inability to face the cruelty: the babies murdered with sharp objects, the heads without bodies and vice versa, the terrorizing of children, the women stripped naked and shot point-blank, the burning of entire families, the mutilations, the rapes, the tortures, and perhaps most of all, the jubilant laughter of the killers as they accomplished their tasks? Letters signed by thousands of artists, writers, academics, philosophers, and journalists in the United States and United Kingdom – Tilda Swinton! Jonathan Lethem! Nan Goldin! – have castigated Israel *without ever mentioning* the Hamas attacks. Why this desperate attempt to 'disappear' October 7, as if it is already ancient – or irrelevant – history? The mealy-mouthed evasions and pretzel-like contortions of the cultural elite are an ignoble thing to behold. Jewish Lives Matter is, clearly, not a rallying cry for many in today's Left.

***

In 1979, leftists who supported the Iranian Revolution had a rude awakening when the mullahs who came to power promptly proceeded to execute leftists, secularists, union organizers, intellectuals, feminists, and everyone else who fit into the enormously capacious category of a counterrevolutionary. There was a lesson here: Activists have the responsibility to know who and what they support, and to separate themselves – openly and decisively – from programs and regimes that are predicated on violence and repression. Similarly, those who imagine that Hamas's slaughters may have promoted 'liberation,' 'justice,' and 'freedom' for Palestinians, as the banners demand, have a big surprise in store.

Unlike Iran in 1979, though, there's no mystery as to what kind of state Hamas, which is an acronym for the Islamic Resistance Movement, aims to create; we need only look at what it already *has* created. This time, no one can plead ignorance. There's little liberation, justice, or freedom to be found in Gaza, where there are no opposition political parties, no elections, and no freedom of the press or of protest. Opponents are arrested, tortured, and sometimes executed. (Yahya Sinwar, a head of Hamas's armed wing, was known as 'the butcher of Khan Younis' for his brutality toward other Palestinians.)[14] Abortion and homosexuality are outlawed (what are those protestors with 'Queers for Palestine' signs thinking?); mentioning trans rights would be unwise. It is legal for husbands to beat their wives, and so-called honor killings go unpunished. The ruling clique is notoriously corrupt, and though Gazans are very poor, Hamas, as an organization, is very rich. 'I Stand with Palestine!' demonstrators and writers proudly proclaim while lauding Hamas for having 'rejuvenated a sense of political possibility'[15] and hastening 'the hour of liberation.'[16] But what, exactly, are they standing for, and what kind of liberation will this be? Aside from the Taliban, Hamas has established the least progressive pseudo-state on Earth. The lesson of Iran has apparently not been learned; history is repeating itself not as farce but as tragedy.

None of this is to underplay the horrible conditions in Gaza, even before the current war. Nor do I minimize the enormous carnage that Israel has rained down on the strip since October 7; the worsening of the Occupation in the West Bank; the increasingly brazen, homicidal violence of the settlers; the denial of Palestinian rights and statehood; and the crazy messianic zealots in the current Israeli government (which will, after the war if not before, in all likelihood fall. Indeed, an absolute precondition for any political settlement between Israel and the Palestinians is the end of the Netanyahu coalition and of Hamas's stranglehold over Gaza.). Much has been written about the crime of the Occupation; much more needs to be.

But Hamas isn't against the Occupation: something it has, perhaps to its credit, made abundantly clear. It has responded to every move toward Palestinian sovereignty, however partial – including Israel's unconditional withdrawal from Gaza in 2005 and the signing of the Oslo Accords – with deepening violence ranging from rocket attacks to suicide bombings. (David Grossman recently told the *New Yorker* that had Hamas turned Gaza into a peaceful and prosperous enclave, as many Palestinians and Israelis had hoped, subsequent withdrawals from West Bank settlements would have proceeded.)[17] What Hamas calls 'usurpation' means Israel itself, regardless of borders. Any political agreement, including two states or even a binational one, is blasphemy: 'So-called peaceful solutions and international conferences' stand 'in contradiction to the principles of the Islamic Resistance Movement,'[18] its founding covenant makes clear; so do its subsequent actions.

The events of October 7 have clarified to Israelis from across the political spectrum – and should to everyone else – just what it means to make Palestine *judenrein*, as Hamas's founding document and its current leaders promise. Indeed, the only way to 'free Palestine from the river to sea,' as thousands of demonstrators worldwide are chanting, is to kill (or at best expel) all the Jews who live there, which is precisely what Hamas openly states is its primary goal. (Rep. Rashida Tlaib recently released a video in which she endorsed this demand, which she then ludicrously tried to spin as 'an aspirational call for ... peaceful coexistence.'[19] Perhaps she imagines that the millions of Israelis expelled from Yemen, Morocco, Iraq, Syria, and a host of other Arab countries will be offered the 'right of return.') Hamas specifies that every Muslim, including women and 'the slave,' is duty-bound to join in the eschatological struggle to cleanse Palestine of 'the Jews,' whom it identifies as the world's most powerful force and mankind's great enemy.[20] October 7 was the practice of that principle.

The insistence of many on the western Left to either conveniently ignore this program or refuse to believe it – despite Hamas's consistent honesty about its aims and means – is a sign of intellectual Orientalism: Palestinians are viewed only as helpless, reactive victims rather than as people who generate ideas and actions. (If you watch the BBC, you will notice that ordinary Gazans are almost never asked about their political views, whereas Israelis from all walks of life are.) But of course Palestinians do construct worldviews and create political programs, and since October 7 Hamas has been especially voluble in explaining its future plans. In late October, Hamas leader Ghazi Hamad affirmed that his organization planned many more October 7-type attacks until it 'annihilates' (his word) Israel;[21] in early November, Hamas spokesman Taher El-Nounou told the *New York Times*, 'I hope that the state of war with Israel will become permanent on all the borders.'[22] This makes calls for a 'mutual ceasefire,' in Tlaib's words, puzzling if not nonsensical. In fact, a ceasefire (as opposed to a humanitarian pause) would be entirely unilateral on Israel's part, which raises the question of why Israel would lay down its arms against a forthrightly eliminationist enemy that holds over 220 hostages. What would happen the day after that one-sided cessation? (Hamas has shot almost 10,000 rockets into Israel, including Tel Aviv, since October 7; in the north, Hezbollah launches daily attacks.) Apparently, Hamas should be allowed to keep its bombs and bomb factories, assault rifles, drones, grenades, missiles, rockets, and tens of thousands of fighters as it plans future mass slaughters. How this will lead to anything approaching peace, as its advocates insist, rather than to war ad infinitum, as Hamas promises, is bewildering. The other option, of course, is that many believe that unending death and destruction are precisely the conditions that Israelis deserve.

***

Hamas does not recognize the category of 'civilian' when it comes to Israelis, which is why a straight-faced, high-level Hamas spokesman could tell Britain's Sky News: 'We didn't kill any civilians.'[23] He wasn't exactly lying; that's just how he sees it. What is less well-known – but is key to understanding the humanitarian calamity in Gaza right now – is that the group does not recognize the category of civilian when it comes to *Palestinians*. Nathan Thrall, formerly head of the International Crisis Group's Arab-Israeli project and a frequent critic of Israel, has pointed out that Hamas undoubtedly knew that the extraordinary cruelty of these attacks would be met with an extraordinarily deadly Israeli response. 'Clearly, this act by Hamas is suicidal,' Thrall said the day after the massacre. 'I think that the attacks are virtually guaranteed to bring civilian deaths [in Palestine] on a greater scale than we have seen.'[24] Amir Tibon, a leftwing journalist who lived in Kibbutz Nahal Oz (where 14 were killed and 5 kidnapped), observed that on October 7, Hamas 'knew they had signed the death certificate of thousands of Gazans. For them it was a price worth paying for the joy of murdering my teenage neighbor and kidnapping children. They knew Gaza would suffer terrible, shocking destruction. They did it anyway.'[25]

Hamas has since confirmed what Thrall and Tibon knew: 'Without a doubt, it was known that the reaction to this great act would be big,' Khalil al-Hayya, a top official, told the *Times*.[26] In fact, Hamas has always found that carnage in Gaza – and the hatred for Israel that it engenders – is among its very best tools. Dead Palestinian babies and dead Israeli babies both serve its purposes, albeit for different reasons. The fact that this is incomprehensibly perverse doesn't make it less true.

Israel is, of course, accountable for the decisions it makes, including its indefensible siege of Gaza, which contradicts international law, and its ground invasion, which doesn't. Though it did not seek this war, it is fully responsible for its actions and their consequences, including unintended ones. Denying food and water to civilians is, quite simply, morally wrong, and no one can deny that the civilian toll in Gaza is appalling. But the enormous numbers of Palestinians who have been, in Hamas's parlance, 'martyred' are no problem, at least for the group's leadership: As its covenant explains, 'Death for the sake of Allah is the loftiest of ... wishes.'[27] That is not outdated rhetoric; as the October 7 attacks unfolded, senior political leader Ismail Haniyeh insisted that 'victory or martyrdom' are the only choices.[28] Ordinary Palestinians, who had no say in the attacks, may see things differently: They are stunned by, and terrified of, the fury of the Israeli response.

Even as the corpses pile up, Hamas remains unconcerned; Hamad has brushed off civilian casualties by explaining, 'We are called a nation of martyrs, and we are proud to sacrifice martyrs.'[29] Moussa Abu Marzouk, another spokesman, has insisted that Hamas bears no responsibility for the fate or well-being of Gazan civilians and has acknowledged that its extensive network of underground tunnels is meant to protect the organization's fighters, not civilians.[30] (Unlike the 'martyrs,' including children, whom Hamas is proud to sacrifice, its fighters are safe underground where they hoard stocks of food, fuel, medicine, and weapons. Much of the senior leadership, however, lives in luxury in Doha, Tehran, and other friendly cities.) Hamas's *desire* for dead Gazans has never been more evident than in this war: It has not joined in the international calls for a humanitarian corridor, and it refuses to release all the kidnapped hostages, which Israel has said is the precondition for ending the siege.

***

There is, and always has been, another tradition, another sense, of what it means to be a 'progressive' and to stand with the oppressed. In 2011, Fred Halliday, a lifelong anti-colonialist who reported for decades from the Arab and Muslim worlds, wrote an essay called 'Terrorism in Historical Perspective.' It is the most intellectually and morally lucid work on the subject that I know. Halliday addressed himself to his comrades on the Left and made a crucial argument: Any movement that claims to represent an oppressed people must act in an ethical way *even if it is not in power and perceives itself as weak*.[31] This is not 'bourgeois moralism'; it is the very basis of universalist ethics.

Oppression is not a carte blanche for severing heads from bodies, shooting hundreds of young festival-goers, bludgeoning people to death, murdering children in front of parents and vice versa, rape, kidnapping babies and the elderly; there is no universe in which these are revolutionary, liberatory, or anti-colonialist acts, much less 'beautiful' ones. Sadism and violence are not synonyms. Sexual torture is not anti-imperialist. An eliminationist program is not a freedom charter. History has proved, again and again, that terrorists and freedom fighters *aren't* the same, which is why the former never achieve anything approaching either liberation or justice. There is no room for 'yes, but.' Why, when it comes to Israelis, is this so hard to understand?

The western Left's response to October 7 will, I believe, be viewed as a moment of moral corruption on a par with the defense of Stalin's purges, Czechoslovakia's anti-Semitic show trials of 1952, the Soviet invasions of Hungary and Czechoslovakia and Poland's anti-Semitic expulsions of 1968, along with the denial of the Khmer Rouge genocide (see under: Chomsky, Noam) and the adulation of China's vicious Cultural Revolution. Since October 7, there have been a handful of liberal and Left writers who have written bravely and honestly: Jonathan Freedland and Howard Jacobson in the *Guardian*, Michelle Goldberg in the *New York Times*, Alan Johnson and Cary Nelson in *Fathom*, Seyla Benhabib in *Medium*. They are, alas, exceptions. Halliday's leftism – the leftism of humane universalism rather than anti-imperialism – is in eclipse, as was Memmi's.

Except in Israel. Somehow, that nation of genocidal-racist-fascist-settler-colonialists has produced a Left that still adheres to the traditional principles of universalist dignity and equality, and that isn't too squeamish to recognize terrorism for what it is. It rejects Manichean reductionism – something it can ill afford – and can therefore hold more than one thought at a time. It understands that Israel is a powerful country *and* is existentially threatened by its enemies. It understands that it is a perpetrator of the Occupation *and* a victim of terrorism. It knows that one can oppose the way in which Netanyahu's government is conducting the war while *also* avowing that a war must be fought. It understands that vanquishing Hamas and defeating Israel's messianic ultra-nationalists – especially those in its government – are not only related but utterly interdependent. It rejects the concept of collective guilt, whether of Israelis or Palestinians. It has a pretty good understanding of what anti-Semitism is. Of necessity, it comprehends tragedy. Its tone is sober rather than histrionic. These are the people who have done more to defend Palestinian rights and promote Palestinian sovereignty than all of the West's self-aggrandizing decolonialists, boycotters, and anti-imperialists combined.

Michael Sfard is one of Israel's most important human rights lawyers; he has spent his life defending Palestinian rights inside and outside of courtrooms. He recently condemned, in the harshest terms, Israel's political response to October 7:

> Israel today is a country and society where … lawmakers from the ruling party are openly and unashamedly calling for a 'second Nakba,' where the defense minister orders a denial of water, food and fuel to millions of civilians, a country whose president, Isaac Herzog, Israel's moderate face, says that all Gazans are responsible for Hamas' crimes ….

The result?

> When the political and military leadership loses all restraint and approves ideas about a massive blow to civilians, we're creating a society where the process of stripping away the humanity of the people on the other side of the border has been completed. And when that happens, the inferno is near.

But he also addressed his (putative) allies:

> Not far from us, on their own way to the black hole, hover those who call themselves members of the 'progressive left.' They're finding it hard to unhesitatingly condemn – and without fleeing to the 'context' – a satanic

orgy of destroying civilian Israeli communities near Gaza, along with their residents. Some are even blabbering something about decolonization being an ugly process; that's what happened in Algeria and Kenya, for example.

Sfard's reaction was clear:

> I read that and die of shame. Maybe you didn't understand, but the struggle to end the occupation and achieve independence for the Palestinian people is part of the universal struggle to defend everyone's human rights, not vice versa.

He continued:

> The idea of the sanctity of human life, the noble idea that every person has basic rights that shouldn't be undermined, isn't a tool for implementing Palestinian independence but the other way around.[32]

The western Left, basking in the safe, prosperous cities of the liberal democracies, lives in a very different world from the one Michael Sfard inhabits. Its moral rot may have suddenly become clear, but an ethical collapse takes time to develop. October 7 reveals the long-simmering theoretical confusions, and the moral void, that dominates many of today's 'progressive' movements. A Left that is fixated on 'decolonization' mistakes a death cult for a liberation movement and is unable to recognize a bloodbath – even one that was filmed, and publicized worldwide, by the killers themselves. A Left that, rightly, demands absolute condemnation of white-nationalist supremacy refuses to disassociate itself from Islamist supremacy. A Left that divides the world between racists and anti-racists and is obsessed with 'people who look like me' can't understand that the clash of two national movements has nothing to do with color or race.

A Left that celebrates diversity vilifies one of the most culturally and ethnically diverse countries in the world. A Left that prizes itself on defending refugees castigates a nation founded almost entirely *by* refugees – among the most immiserated and persecuted in history – as 'settler-colonial.' A Left that divides the world between noble 'native' peoples and the aliens who pollute them reproduces the neo-fascist worldview of the far-Right, from Donald Trump to Marine Le Pen. A Left that lauds intersectionality hasn't noticed that Hamas's axis of support consists of Iran, famous most recently for killing hundreds of protestors demanding women's freedom; the homicidal dictatorship of Syria's Bashar al-Assad; and Hezbollah, another fundamentalist Islamic group that is dedicated to Israel's destruction and that terrorizes, and sometimes assassinates, fellow Lebanese who oppose it. What kind of Left gets into bed with such forces? Nor has it noticed that, since October 7, ISIS and al-Qaeda have urged Muslims to step up 'operations against the Jews' in solidarity with Hamas.[33]

And so, as always, the eternally vexing Jewish Question emerges, though many on the Left seem to think it's been answered. A Left that has spent years, and spilled mountains of ink, tediously insisting that anti-Zionism cannot morph into anti-Semitism is unable to discern, much less clearly denounce, a militia of *avowed* Jew-killers. A Left that sees systemic racism in every nook and cranny – and in every (white) heart – can't recognize the systemic anti-Semitism that results in mass murder. 'I killed 10 Jews with my own hands!' a Hamas terrorist exulted as he called his parents, in the midst of the October attacks, to tell them the good news and send photos to prove it.[34] That cry – both modern and ancient – must also be seen as a root cause of October 7; that, too, is a key part of its context.

Individually and collectively, Israeli leftists have expressed their sorrow, their shock, and their anger at the western Left's betrayal. Crucially, they have tried to educate their supposed comrades about what a true Left response – to both the Occupation and October 7 – must be. A group statement signed by some of Israel's most prominent intellectuals read in part:

> Many of our peers worldwide have expressed strong opposition to Hamas's attack and have offered unambiguous support for its victims. Prominent voices in the Arab world, too, have made it clear that there is no justification for sadistic murder of innocent people. However, to our dismay, some elements within the global left, individuals who were, until now, our political partners, have reacted with indifference to these horrific events and sometimes even justified Hamas's actions .... And there are even those – no small number – for whom the darkest day in our society's history was a cause for celebration.
>
> This array of responses surprised us. We never imagined that individuals on the left, advocates of equality, freedom, justice, and welfare, would reveal such extreme moral insensitivity and political recklessness.... We emphasize: there is no contradiction between staunchly opposing the Israeli subjugation and occupation of Palestinians and unequivocally condemning brutal acts of violence against innocent civilians. In fact, every consistent leftist must hold both positions simultaneously.[35]

Sociologist Eva Illouz was even more blunt. She closed a recent article in *Haaretz* with this farewell note:

> Many Arabs, within Israel and without, have shown the compassion the doctrinal left has so shockingly lacked. They have stood by our side. It is them with whom we must build a party of humanity determined to bring justice and peace. The global left has made itself irrelevant from now on.[36]

The Left in Israel, unlike the global Left, recognizes that appeasing will not bring peace to Israelis or justice to Palestinians. 'A country that doesn't kill the people who tried to murder my daughters, and those who sent them, has lost its right to exist,' Tibon wrote.[37] Civilians in Gaza must be protected whenever possible – something that is clearly not happening – but Hamas's concealment of fighters and weapons within the civilian population and civilian sites makes this exceedingly difficult. Postwar, new political landscapes will emerge, though only a fool would predict what they'll be. (One thing is clear: The political leaderships of both peoples have led them, and each other, to ruin.) October 7, Tibon wrote, 'hasn't changed my belief, based on a cold, calculated reading of reality, that in the long run we must find ways to share this land …. But first we must survive.'[38] It has become obvious that there are many on the Left who dispute that last sentence.

Notes

1 A version of this essay appeared in "Quillette," November 18, 2023.
2 Memmi. A. (1967) *The Colonizer and the Colonized*. Translated by Howard Greenfield. Boston: Beacon Press, pp. 30–31.
3 Sid-Ahmed, M. (1976) *After the Guns Fall Silent: Peace or Armageddon in the Middle East*. Translated by Maissa Talaat. London: Croom Helm, p. 127.
4 Halliday, F. "On the PFLP and the September Crisis: Interview with Ghassan Kannafani." *New Left Review* (May-June 1971), p. 50.
5 https://twitter.com/HeidiBachram/status/1711072521800360252?s=20; accessed October 8, 2023.
6 Ali, T. "Uprising in Palestine." *New Left Review*, October 7, 2023; https://newleftreview.org/sidecar/posts/uprising-in-palestine; accessed October 8, 2023.
7 Iraqi, A. "Get Out of There Now," *London Review of Books*, October 10, 2023; https://www.lrb.co.uk/blog/2023/october/get-out-of-there-now; accessed October 11, 2023.
8 Winant, G. "On Mourning and Statehood: A Response to Joshua Leifer," *Dissent*, October 13, 2023; https://www.dissentmagazine.org/online_articles/a-response-to-joshua-leifer/; accessed October 13, 2023.
9 Massad, J. "Just Another Battle or the Palestinian War of Liberation?", *The Electronic Intifada*, October 8, 2023; https://electronicintifada.net/content/just-another-battle-or-palestinian-war-liberation/38661; accessed October 9, 2023.
10 https://www.adl.org/resources/blog/anti-israel-activists-celebrate-hamas-attacks-have-killed-hundreds-israelis; accessed October 14, 2023.
11 Eptstein, R. and Huynh, A., "Democrats Split Over Israel as the Young, Diverse Left Rages at Biden," *New York Times*, October 28, 2023; https://www.nytimes.com/2023/10/27/us/politics/biden-democrats-israel-2024.html; accessed October 28, 2023.
12 Maltz, J. "Columbia Faculty Statement Terming Hamas Massacre 'Military Action' Draws Fury," *Haaretz*, October 30, 2023; https://www.haaretz.com/us-news/2023-10-30/ty-article/.premium/columbia-faculty-statement-terming-hamas-massacre-military-action-draws-fury/0000018b-80ae-d4a8-a3cf-bcaf65880000; accessed October 31, 2023.
13 "An Open Letter from Participants in the Palestine Festival of Literature," *New York Review of Books*, October 14, 2023; https://www.nybooks.com/online/2023/10/14/an-open-letter-from-participants-in-the-palestine-festival-of-literature/; accessed October 15, 2023.

14 Hubbard, B. and Abi-Habib, M., "Behind Hamas's Bloody Gambit to Create a 'Permanent' State of War," *New York Times*, November 9, 2023; https://www.nytimes.com/2023/11/08/world/middleeast/hamas-israel-gaza-war.html; accessed November 9, 2023.

15 Iraqi, A. "A Psychological Barrier Has Just Been Shattered in Israel-Palestine," *+972*, October 11, 2023; https://www.972mag.com/hamas-october-attack-gaza-barrier/; accessed October 13, 2023.

16 https://www.adl.org/resources/blog/anti-israel-activists-celebrate-hamas-attacks-have-killed-hundreds-israelis; accessed October 15, 2023.

17 Remnick, D. "In the Cities of Killing," *The New Yorker*, October 28, 2023; https://www.newyorker.com/magazine/2023/11/06/israel-gaza-war-hamas; accessed October 29, 2023.

18 Hamas Covenant, 1988: https://avalon.law.yale.edu/20th_century/hamas.asp; accessed October 12, 2023.

19 Guo, K. "Rashida Tlaib Posts Video Accusing Biden of 'Genocide,'" *New York Times*, November 3, 2023; www.nytimes.com/2023/11/03/world/middleeast/rashida-tlaib-biden-israel-palestinians.html; accessed November 3, 2023.

20 Hamas Covenant, 1988, https://avalon.law.yale.edu/20th_century/hamas.asp; accessed October 12, 2023.

21 "Hamas Official: We Will Repeat October 7 Attacks Until Israel is Annihilated," *Haaretz*, November 1, 2023; https://www.haaretz.com/israel-news/2023-11-01/ty-article/hamas-official-we-will-repeat-october-7-attacks-until-israel-is-annihilated/0000018b-8b9d-db7e-af9b-ebdfbee90000; accessed November 1, 2023.

22 Hubbard, B. and Abi-Habib, M. "Behind Hamas's Bloody Gambit to Create a 'Permanent' State of War," *New York Times*, November 9, 2023; https://www.nytimes.com/2023/11/08/world/middleeast/hamas-israel-gaza-war.html; accessed November 9, 2023.

23 https://news.sky.com/video/israel-hamas-war-we-have-not-killed-any-civilians-hamas-official-tells-sky-news-12981219; accessed October 10, 2023.

24 Chotiner, I. "Could the Attack on Israel Spell the End of Hamas?", *The New Yorker*, October 8, 2023; https://www.haaretz.com/israel-news/2023-11-07/ty-article/.premium/hamas-tried-to-kill-my-children-on-october-7-it-knew-what-would-happen-next-in-gaza/0000018b-a985-d530-a5df-e9efc0e40000; accessed October 8, 2023.

25 Tibon, A. "When Hamas Tried to Kill My Children on October 7 They Knew What Would Happen Next in Gaza," *Haaretz*, November 7, 2023; https://www.haaretz.com/israel-news/2023-11-07/ty-article/.premium/hamas-tried-to-kill-my-children-on-october-7-it-knew-what-would-happen-next-in-gaza/0000018b-a985-d530-a5df-e9efc0e40000; accessed November 8, 2023.

26 Hubbard, B. and Abi-Habib, M. "Behind Hamas's Bloody Gambit to Create a 'Permanent' State of War," *New York Times*, November 9, 2023; https://www.nytimes.com/2023/11/08/world/middleeast/hamas-israel-gaza-war.html; accessed November 9, 2023.

27 Hamas Covenant, 1988, https://avalon.law.yale.edu/20th_century/hamas.asp; accessed October 12, 2023.

28 Levitt, M. "The War Hamas Always Wanted," *Foreign Affairs*, October 11, 2023; https://www.foreignaffairs.com/israel/war-hamas-always-wanted; accessed October 12, 2023.

29 *Times of Israel* Staff. "Hamas says purpose of massacres was a 'permanent' state of war on Israel's borders," November 8, 2023; https://www.timesofisrael.com/hamas-says-it-staged-massacres-to-cause-permanent-state-of-war-on-israels-borders/; accessed November 9, 2023.

30 Pacchiani, G. "Top Hamas Official Declares Group Is Not Responsible for Defending Gazan Civilians," *Times of Israel*, October 31, 2023; https://www.timesofisrael.com/top-hamas-official-claims-group-is-not-responsible-for-defending-gazan-civilians/; accessed November 1, 2023.

31 See Halliday, F. "Terrorism in Historical Perspective," *OpenDemocracy*, May 2, 2011; https://www.opendemocracy.net/en/article_1865jsp/; accessed May 5, 2011.

32 Sfard, M. "In Gaza, Israel is Racing to the Moral Abyss," *Haaretz*, October 23, 2023; https://www.haaretz.com/israel-news/2023-10-23/ty-article-opinion/.premium/ in-gaza-israel-is-racing-to-the-moral-abyss/0000018b-57d1-d8e2-a1eb-f7d7dc100000 accessed; accessed October 23, 2023.

33 Sullivan, E. "F.B.I. Says Israel-Hamas War Raises Potential for Attacks Against Americans," *New York Times*, October 31, 2023; https://www.nytimes. com/2023/10/31/us/politics/wray-threats-us.html; accessed October 31, 2023.

34 Wood, G. "A Record of Pure, Predatory Sadism," *The Atlantic*, October 23, 2023; https://www.theatlantic.com/ideas/archive/2023/10/why-israeli-officials-screened-footage-hamas-attack/675735/; accessed October 25, 2023.

35 "Statement on behalf of Israel and Israel-based progressives and peace activists," October 17, 2023; https://www.theatlantic.com/ideas/archive/2023/10/why-israeli-officials-screened-footage-hamas-attack/675735/; accessed October 20, 2023.

36 Illouz, E. "The Global Left's Reaction to October 7 Threatens the Fight Against the Occupation," *Haaretz*, November 2, 2023; https://www.haaretz.com/opinion/ 2023-11-02/ty-article-opinion/.premium/the-global-lefts-reaction-to-october-7-threatens-the-fight-against-the-occupation/0000018b-8b8d-d7a8-afcf-abaf5d670000; accessed November 4, 2023.

37 Tibon, A. "When Hamas Tried to Kill My Children on October 7 They Knew What Would Happen Next in Gaza," *Haaretz*, November 7, 2023; https://www.haaretz. com/israel-news/2023-11-07/ty-article/.premium/hamas-tried-to-kill-my-children-on-october-7-it-knew-what-would-happen-next-in-gaza/0000018b-a985-d530-a5df-e9efc0e40000; accessed November 8, 2023.

38 Ibid.

7 Rain of Ashes Over Elite American Universities

Günther Jikeli[1]

What does humanity even mean after the 7th of October? '*Humanityyyyyy, we certainly could use a little bit of it. Since the attack of Hamas, I no longer know what this is supposed to be,*' writes Elfriede Jelinek, winner of the Nobel Prize for Literature after deleting all her other work from her website. And indeed, the massacre, which can hardly be put into words, as well as the lack of condemnation in its aftermath and the many relativizations of what happened, put into serious question whether there is even such a thing as a common humanity. The reactions at some American universities were particularly shocking.

Already on October 7, students at Harvard, one of America's most elite universities, came together to express their unreserved solidarity with the Palestinians. '*We [...] hold the Israeli regime entirely responsible for all unfolding violence,*' they began in a statement drafted by the Palestine Solidarity Committee and co-signed by 33 other campus organizations. '*[T]he massacres in Gaza have already commenced [...]. The apartheid regime is the only one to blame. Israeli violence has structured every aspect of Palestinian existence for 75 years [...]. The coming days will require a firm stand against colonial retaliation. We call on the Harvard community to take action to stop the ongoing annihilation of Palestinians,*' it continued, all on October 7, mind you.[2]

Not a word about Hamas, which makes no secret of its murderous and uncompromising fight against the Jews.[3] But all the keywords of the anticolonial struggle were there. Israel was accused of apartheid and the annihilation of the Palestinians, and this on the day Hamas carried out a pogrom that can be described as genocide according to the definition of the UN Genocide Convention.[4]

A crazy exception and a slip-up? After a public outcry, including among potential employers of prospective junior lawyers, especially large law firms, and a doxing campaign that published the names of the signatories, some cosignatories distanced themselves from the statement. Just a few days later, however, Brown University's Students for Justice in Palestine group released a very similar statement, co-signed by 50 groups. '*We, the undersigned, hold*

DOI: 10.4324/9781003497424-7

the Israeli regime and its allies unequivocally responsible for all suffering and loss of life, Palestinian or Israeli,' it read and pledged *'solidarity with Palestinian resistance against Israeli occupation.'*[5] In other words, support for Hamas.

Demonstrations of 'resistance' took place at many universities in the week after the massacre. On October 12, five days after the mass killings, Students for Justice in Palestine (SJP) called for 'resistance' rallies at universities, and many followed their lead. In their published toolkit, the national SJP organization celebrated the *'surprise operation against the Zionist enemy'* and emphasized that *'settlers are not 'civilians' in the sense of international law, because they are military assets used to ensure continued control over stolen Palestinian land.'*[6] A second round of organized student protests took place on 25 October. There were antisemitic incidents.[7]

Not only could the antisemitic call for ethnic cleansing, 'Palestine will be free, from the river to the sea' be heard and read, but Jewish students were also physically harassed and threatened in some places. Protesters at the Cooper Union in New York, who chanted *'Free Palestine,'* banged on locked library doors behind which Jewish students had to hide. At a protest at New York University, two students were seen holding signs reading *'Keep the world clean,'* alongside a drawing of a Star of David in a trash can. At the University of Wisconsin, Milwaukee, Students for Democratic Society called for a strike and emphasized in statements on social media that *'Zionism has no place on our campus'* and used the hashtag *'#ZionismOffCampus.'* Students at George Washington University projected *'Glory To Our Martyrs'* and *'Free Palestine from the river to the sea'* on the outside walls of the university library.[8] Students from the University of North Carolina called on the university to boycott all Israeli companies and 'companies that have supported Israel.'[9] Others staged a boycott of Starbucks and McDonald's for what they said was company support of Israel.[10]

A speaker at the University of Washington explained, *'We don't want Israel to exist. We don't want these Zionist counter-protesters to exist.'*[11] A speech was also given at the University of Minnesota that explicitly called for the destruction of Israel. *'We must have as the aim the destruction of the imperialist Zionist regime for a successful intifada.'* To which the crowd chanted: *'Intifada until victory! There is only one solution: Intifada, revolution.'*[12] At Cornell University, a mentally disturbed student was charged with threatening to kill Jewish students in a kosher restaurant, which consequently had to close temporarily. In online messages, he threatened to *'stab'* and *'slit the throat'* of any Jewish males he sees on campus, to rape and throw off a cliff any Jewish females, to behead any Jewish babies, and to *'bring an assault rifle to campus and shoot all you pig jews.'*[13] At some universities, an antizionist mob emerged that threatened to turn violent against Jews at any moment.

Posters with pictures of the hostages kidnapped by Hamas were often graffitied or torn down. The fact that Israelis are still victims and are threatened with death simply does not fit into the binary worldview. It must be removed from view. The majority of Jewish students surveyed at over 50 universities in late November/early December expressed concern about the hostility toward Jews on their campus, with over 80 percent at some universities. Between 52 and 73 percent said they had seen antisemitic images on campus. Depending on the university, between 14 and 24 percent of Jewish students stated that they had personally been the victim of harassment or insults on campus, and between 26 and 35 percent on social media.[14]

There was also little empathy from many professors, neither for the Israeli victims nor for Jewish students. A Jewish student at Indiana University showed me a photo she had taken of one of my colleagues tearing down a poster of an Israeli hostage. There were not only statements by individual professors justifying the massacre, but also jointly written open letters insisting on the 'right to resist.' According to a letter from 144 Columbia University professors, *'one could regard the events of October 7 ... as an occupied people exercising a right to resist violent and illegal occupation.'*[15] At the City University of New York, more than 200 faculty members downplayed the massacre, euphemistically calling it a *'military operation by Hamas.'*[16]

Most university leaders, who were not at a loss for clear words when it came to other global political or social issues, such as the war against Ukraine or the anti-racist protests after George Floyd's death, found it difficult to name the massacre or pogrom in Israel as such and to condemn expressions of solidarity with the *'Palestinian resistance,'* meaning Hamas, as well as antisemitic slogans at rallies at their universities. The stark contrast and double standard became apparent and measurable.[17] To the despair of Jewish students and faculty, in many places, it took massive pressure from alumni, donors, and politicians before there was a public statement from the university presidents condemning the Hamas pogrom and the antisemitic incidents on campus. When antisemitism was condemned, it was often in the same breath as condemning bigotry against Muslims.[18]

When the presidents of three of the most prestigious colleges in the world, namely Harvard, MIT, and University of Pennsylvania, were invited to a congressional hearing in early December 2023, it became clear how unprepared university leaders were to offer meaningful answers. Their failure to unequivocally condemn calls for genocide against the Jews on their campuses, even after repeated requests to do so, and to make it clear that such hostile language runs counter to the rules of conduct at their universities, left millions of viewers worldwide bewildered and appalled. The Republican-led commission that convened the hearing summarized, *'Each came prepared with nearly identical, canned remarks. Each condemned antisemitism, the bare minimum. Each equated antisemitism with less pervasive anti-Palestinian sentiments. Each made promises to establish do-nothing task forces.'*[19] But not only Republicans were outraged. There was also clear condemnation from the White House[20] and a bipartisan resolution of the House of Representatives condemned the statements as '*evasive and dismissive.*'[21] The Ministry of Education is now investigating dozens of cases in which universities might have discriminated against students because of their ancestry, which could lead to severe cuts in public funding.[22]

At many American universities, especially at elite universities, there seems to be a climate in which it is difficult to show empathy with the Jewish-Israeli victims of a pogrom and to unequivocally condemn the act and the perpetrators. Resistance '*by any means necessary,*' as was written on some posters at pro-Palestinian demonstrations,[23] apparently includes pogroms. Critical questions from outside are interpreted by professors as an attempt to restrict freedom of speech and academic freedom. However, this is rarely the case, at least so far, even if it is true that Republican politicians are trying to exploit the issue for partisan purposes and attack universities that are perceived as left-liberal.[24]

How could it come to this? Two factors appear to be particularly important. Both are especially pronounced at elite universities. First, since the 1960s, numerous study programs have been established in the humanities that are committed to postcolonialism, in the tradition of Edward Said, among others. Postcolonialism accuses the West of having a binary view of the world, which it itself propagates in reverse. This has led to the spread of a dogmatic and at the same time diffuse postmodernism and postcolonialism with fragmentary references to Critical Theory, which solidified into a binary worldview among some teachers and students. The world is divided into oppressor and oppressed peoples, into the privileged and the disadvantaged. Social relations are perceived exclusively as power relations, whereby one's own position is regarded as powerless – even at elite universities. The acquisition of knowledge and learning at university are also only seen as an instrument for maintaining power.

Resistance must be staged. Against whom? Against imperialism, the state, the system, they say. But this does not mean all states, not all imperialisms, not all patriarchal structures, at least not if they are outside Europe or North America. 'Resistance' primarily refers to antagonism against the United States and Israel, the latter being a socially easier target. The contradictions are obvious. Antisemitism offers itself here as a masterful glue to hold this worldview together.

Interestingly, part of the thought patterns anchored in today's postcolonialism can be traced back to the Soviet Union's anti-Zionist propaganda campaign from 1967 until shortly before its collapse. As Izabella Tabarovsky demonstrates, the radical anti-Zionism that was deliberately crafted as a propaganda tool during this period associated Israel with racism, settler colonialism, imperialism, fascism, National Socialism, and apartheid.[25] The slogans that can be heard at anti-Israeli demonstrations today are strikingly similar to those of that time, except that today they are propagated at elite universities and in mass rallies in the West and not just in left-wing splinter groups.

Drawing on the Soviet anti-imperialism and anti-Zionism campaigns, influential thinkers in the anti-racist and feminist movement such as Angela Davis linked or equated the anti-racist struggle of African-Americans with the struggle of Palestinians under the slogan of intersectionality and successfully popularized this equation in the Black Lives Matter movement.[26] The theories of intersectionality and Critical Race Theory, which are also in the tradition of postmodernism and postcolonialism, were able to correctly describe forms of discrimination that persist even after the successes of the civil rights movement. However, they have prepared the ground for an ethnic-identitarian activism that demands stereotyped thinking.[27]

According to this notion, only members of their own group can really understand the discrimination directed against them; an awareness must therefore be created not of class but of racial identity, and all those affected by discrimination must show solidarity for each other's fight against oppression. However, discrimination and oppression are diffusely described as systemic and are thought of almost exclusively as the impact of white privilege and power. The binary post-colonialist worldview is racially charged inversely. Ethnic and other minorities are seen per se as oppressed and good, whites as oppressors and bad, unless they acknowledge their privileges and join the chorus of postcolonialist intersectionality. Jews are not perceived as victims of oppression or discrimination, despite or perhaps because of their being on the receiving end for centuries of persecution, but as privileged whites.[28] From there, it is only a small step to rail against 'Jewish privilege' – a prominent theme in *Mein Kampf.*

In addition to these ideological influences and the excesses of postmodern and postcolonial theories, the multi-billion-dollar influence of Arab investors is also evident.[29] First Saudi Arabia and, after September 11th, increasingly Qatar, invested large sums in the development of Middle Eastern Studies and other university-based programs, which successfully contributed to the establishment of anti-Israeli positions in the humanities. The number of antisemitic incidents on campus has been shown to correlate strongly with the amount of foreign investment in universities, especially when the investment comes from Middle Eastern countries.[30] The influence of targeted propaganda by organizations such as the Boycott, Disinvestment, and Sanctions (BDS) Campaign and Students for Justice in Palestine (SJP) cannot be overlooked either. Both are present at many universities and have formed student groups there. Since October 7, local SJP groups have organized protests at many universities in which Hamas was celebrated as a resistance movement. SJP also made a name for itself in the past with anti-Israeli actions.[31] A drastic increase in anti-Israeli activities has already been recorded since 2021, often involving SJP groups and the anti-Zionist organization Jewish Voice for Peace (JVP).[32] The latter's involvement is often misused to protect against allegations of antisemitism. Lobby organizations with ties to Hamas, such as American Muslims for Palestine and the Council on American-Islamic Relations (CAIR),[33] are more active in the background at universities and try to stifle criticism of Islamist positions with accusations of Islamophobia. CAIR was a regular partner in official strategies to combat discrimination, including the White House's strategy to combat antisemitism, until a speech by its director became public in which he described the October 7 massacre as self-defense by Palestinians.[34]

The anti-Zionist anti-colonialist worldview, in which there are only oppressors and oppressed and in which organizations such as the SJP must not be criticized because they belong to the oppressed of this earth, seems to be so widespread and deeply rooted among some students and also in parts of the professoriate that even such a barbaric and brutal pogrom as that of October 7 does not call this worldview into question.

It is difficult to say how widespread such worldviews are. Surveys suggest that these are no longer minority opinions, at least not among younger people. It is worth taking a closer look at those surveys.

The Center for American Political Studies at Harvard conducts monthly surveys on various political topics. From October to December 2023, participants were asked whether they tended to give more support to Israel or Hamas. The vast majority sided with Israel, but just under a fifth supported Hamas. Among 18–24-year-olds, however, almost half of respondents supported Hamas. And more than half of this age group agreed that 'the killing of 1,200 Israeli civilians by Hamas and the kidnapping of another 250 civilians can be justified by the suffering of Palestinians.'[35] In late November/early December, the Pew Research Center conducted a representative survey. Far more Americans (65 percent) blamed Hamas for the conflict than the Israeli government (35 percent). Among young people under 30, however, the difference was small (46–42 percent). Moreover, about half of the population was very or extremely concerned about the possible increase in violence against Jews in the United States, roughly evenly split between Republican and Democrat supporters. However, Democrats, unlike Republicans, were even more concerned about the possible increase in violence against Muslims.[36] In mid-December, registered voters were surveyed for *The New York Times*. Overall, 44 percent said Israel should stop its military action to avoid civilian casualties. The percentage was nearly 10 percent higher among voters with a college degree. Among those under 30, the figure was 67 percent. Criticism of Israel was particularly high among TikTok users.[37]

There are certainly manifold reasons why some students in the United States are not only critical of Israel but also take a stand for Hamas and try to legitimize its inhuman and barbaric violence. Ignorance also seems to be a factor. Some people truly do not seem to know which river and which sea the Hamas slogans refer to.[38] Perhaps ignorance, even at elite universities, makes people more susceptible to phrases of grossly simplistic post-colonial ideologies and Islamist propaganda – whether at university or on TikTok. However, it can be assumed that now, at the latest after the public discussions, most of those who are still kowtowing to Hamas in the name of resistance are at least condoning the murder of Jews and do not care about their barbarous and genocidal violence. Humanity has become a rain of ashes because of Hamas, writes Elfriede Jelinek. The rain is falling abundantly at elite universities.

Notes

1 A shorter version of this chapter was published in German in Die Tageszeitung on December 5, 2023. It is republished here with permission.

2 Hill, J.S. and Orakwue, N.L. (2023) 'Harvard Student Groups Face Intense Backlash for Statement Calling Israel "Entirely Responsible" for Hamas Attack', *The Harvard Crimson*, 10 October. Available at: https://www.thecrimson.com/article/2023/10/10/psc-statement-backlash/ (Accessed: 18 December 2023).

3 Hoffman, B. (2023) 'Understanding Hamas's Genocidal Ideology', *The Atlantic*, 10 October. Available at: https://www.theatlantic.com/international/archive/2023/10/hamas-covenant-israel-attack-war-genocide/675602/ (Accessed: 22 December 2023).

4 'Dozens of International Legal Experts: Hamas Committed War Crimes, Crimes against Humanity' (2023) *Israel National News*. Available at: https://www.israelnationalnews.com/news/378520 (Accessed: 18 December 2023).

5 Brown Students for Justice in Palestine (2023) *Brown Students for Justice in Palestine's Statement on the Recent Events in Palestine, Instagram*. Available at: https://www.instagram.com/p/CyRiOLyp2Ge/ (Accessed: 23 December 2023).

6 National Students for Justice in Palestine (2023) *Day of Resistance Toolkit*. Available at: https://dw-wp-production.imgix.net/2023/10/DAY-OF-RESISTANCE-TOOLKIT.pdf (Accessed: 17 December 2023).

7 Anti-Defamation League (2023c) *Walkouts at U.S. Colleges Demand End to Aid for Israel, Include Support for Terror*. Available at: https://www.adl.org/resources/blog/walkouts-us-colleges-demand-end-aid-israel-include-support-terror (Accessed: 18 December 2023).

8 Phillips, A. (2023) 'George Washington University Pro-Palestinian Message Sparks Outrage', *Newsweek*, 25 October. Available at: https://www.newsweek.com/george-washington-university-pro-palestinian-message-outrage-1837735 (Accessed: 22 December 2023).

9 'UNC Students Hold Sit-In Protest Outside Chancellor's Office in Support of Palestinians' (2023) *ABC11*. Available at: https://abc11.com/palestine-unc-students-war-protest-israel-gaza/13981013/ (Accessed: 22 December 2023).

10 Young, J. and Lewis, E. (2023) 'Students Call for Boycotting Starbucks, McDonald's Over Israel-Gaza War – The Hilltop', *The Hilltop*, 14 November. Available at: https://thehilltoponline.com/2023/11/14/students-call-for-boycotting-starbucks-mcdonalds-over-israel-gaza-war/ (Accessed: 22 December 2023).

11 Rantz, J. (2023) 'UW Seattle Activist Declares 'We Don't Want Israel to Exist'', *MyNorthwest.com*. Available at: https://mynorthwest.com/3936644/rantz-uw-seattle-activist-declares-we-dont-want-israel-to-exist/ (Accessed: 20 December 2023).

12 Anti-Defamation League (2023c) *Walkouts at U.S. Colleges Demand End to Aid for Israel, Include Support for Terror*. Available at: https://www.adl.org/resources/blog/walkouts-us-colleges-demand-end-aid-israel-include-support-terror (Accessed: 18 December 2023).

13 United States Attorney's Office. Northern District of New York (2023) 'Cornell Student Arrested for Making Online Threats to Jewish Students on Campus', *United States Department of Justice*. Available at: https://www.justice.gov/usao-ndny/pr/cornell-student-arrested-making-online-threats-jewish-students-campus (Accessed: 20 December 2023).

14 G Wright, G. *et al.* (2023) *In the Shadow of War: Hotspots of Antisemitism on US College Campuses.* Available at: https://www.brandeis.edu/cmjs/research/antisemitism/hotspots-2023-report1.html (Accessed: 20 December 2023).

15 Franke, K. *et al.* (2023) *An Open Letter from Columbia University and Barnard College Faculty in Defense of Robust Debate About the History and Meaning of the War in Israel/Gaza.* Available at: https://docs.google.com/document/d/1cVLg6 RTnqd2BTzuouWbfACnFEex7GQeImDZJnMlUReM/preview (Accessed: 18 December 2023).

16 Jawad, A. *et al.* (2023) *CUNY Faculty and Staff Reject the Palestine Exception to Free Speech.* Available at: https://docs.google.com/document/d/e/2PACX-1vT1FLJtSCq9kn8uTAwNLlr4V9kkoGWxGsS6PPTwuaDNesQHbprxwi AQhWsv4MBsOpe5vyZBaJsAeyx7/pub?urp=gmail_link (Accessed: 18 December 2023).

17 AMCHA Initiative (2023) *Selective Sympathy: The Double Standard in Confronting Jewish Student Trauma & Antisemitism. After the October 7th Massacre.* Available at: https://t.co/qH1ET7rbCw (Accessed: 20 December 2023).

18 The juxtaposition of anti-Muslim hatred to antisemitism has the effect of framing antisemitism as a conflict between Jews and Muslims, thereby exonerating the non-Jewish and non-Muslim majority. This is exacerbated by the use of the misleading term Islamophobia, which blurs the distinction between irrational hatred of Muslims, which should be unequivocally condemned, and criticism of Islamist ideology, which should be allowed, especially in this context where Hamas slogans have been used.

19 Committee on Education & the Workforce, U.S. House of Representatives (2023a) *Hearing Recap: College Presidents Edition.* Available at: https://edworkforce.house.gov/news/documentsingle.aspx?DocumentID=409831 (Accessed: 20 December 2023).

20 Lonas, L. (2023) 'White House Weighs in University Presidents' Remarks at Antisemitism Hearing: "Unbelievable"', *The Hill*, 6 December. Available at: https://thehill.com/homenews/education/4345708-white-house-university-antisemitism/ (Accessed: 20 December 2023).

21 Committee on Education & the Workforce, U.S. House of Representatives (2023b) *House Passes Resolution to Condemn Testimony of Gay, Magill, and Kornbluth.* Available at: https://edworkforce.house.gov/news/documentsingle. aspx?DocumentID=409903 (Accessed: 20 December 2023).

22 U.S. Department of Education (2023) *U.S. Department of Education's Office for Civil Rights Announces List of Open Title VI Shared Ancestry Investigations of Institutions of Higher Education and K-12 Schools.* Available at: https://www.ed.gov/news/press-releases/us-department-educations-office-civil-rights-announces-list-open-title-vi-shared-ancestry-investigations-institutions-higher-education-and-k-12-schools (Accessed: 20 December 2023).

23 Barone, C. (2023) 'Suspended at Columbia, Pro-Palestinian Protesters Fill Streets Outside Campus Gates', *The Forward*, 15 November. Available at: https://forward.com/fast-forward/570001/sjp-jvp-suspended-columbia-pro-palestinian-protesters-broadway/ (Accessed: 18 December 2023); Rigolizzo, J. (2023) *'By Any Means Necessary': UW Madison Students Chant Pro-Hamas Slogans at Campus Rally, Campus Reform.* Available at: https://www.campusreform.org/article/by-any-means-necessary-uw-madison-students-chant-pro-hamas-slogans-at-campus-rally/24160 (Accessed: 18 December 2023).

24 Pew Research Center (2019) 'The Growing Partisan Divide in Views of Higher Education', *Pew Research Center's Social & Demographic Trends Project*, 19 August. Available at: https://www.pewresearch.org/social-trends/2019/08/19/the-growing-partisan-divide-in-views-of-higher-education-2/ (Accessed: 20 December 2023).

25 Tabarovsky, I. (2019) 'Soviet Anti-Zionism and Contemporary Left Antisemitism', *Fathom* [Preprint]. Available at: https://fathomjournal.org/soviet-anti-zionism-and-contemporary-left-antisemitism/ (Accessed: 13 August 2020).

26 Blackmer, C.E. (2022) *Queering Anti-Zionism: Academic Freedom, LGBTQ Intellectuals, and Israel/Palestine Campus Activism*. Wayne State University Press, p. 82.

27 This is often pejoratively referred to as wokeism. Yascha Mounk uses the more neutral term identity synthesis. Mounk, Y. (2023) *The Identity Trap: A Story of Ideas and Power in Our Time*. New York: Penguin Press. Max Horkheimer and Theodor Adorno made a similar observation during fascism when they wrote their book "Dialectic of the Enlightenment," including the chapter "Elements of Antisemitism." They called this stereotyped thinking "ticket thinking." Horkheimer, M. and Adorno, T.W. (1972) *Dialectic of Enlightenment*. London: Verso.

28 Ahmari, S. (2018) 'Why Postmodern Intersectionality Imperils Israel and Jews', *Commentary Magazine*, 20 March. Available at: https://www.commentary.org/sohrab-ahmari/why-postmodern-intersectionality-imperils-israel-and-jews/ (Accessed: 21 December 2023).

29 Small, C.A. and Bass, M. (2020) *Examining Undocumented Foreign Funding of American Universities: Implications for Education and Rising Antisemitism. Volume II*. Institute for the Study of Global Antisemitism and Policy. Available at: https://isgap.org/post/2020/09/volume-ii-examining-undocumented-foreign-funding-of-american-universities-implications-for-education-and-rising-antisemitism/ (Accessed: 20 December 2023); Small, C.A. *et al.* (2023) *The Corruption of The American Mind: How Foreign Funding in U.S. Higher Education By Authoritarian Regimes, Widely Undisclosed, Predicts Erosion Of Democratic Norms And Antisemitic Incidents On Campus*. Network Contagion Research Institute and Institute for the Study of Global Antisemitism and Policy. Available at: https://networkcontagion.us/reports/11-6-23-the-corruption-of-the-american-mind/ (Accessed: 18 December 2023).

30 Small, C.A. *et al.* (2023) *The Corruption of The American Mind: How Foreign Funding in U.S. Higher Education By Authoritarian Regimes, Widely Undisclosed, Predicts Erosion Of Democratic Norms And Antisemitic Incidents On Campus*. Network Contagion Research Institute and Institute for the Study of Global Antisemitism and Policy. Available at: https://networkcontagion.us/reports/11-6-23-the-corruption-of-the-american-mind/ (Accessed: 18 December 2023).

31 Anti-Defamation League (2023b) *Students for Justice in Palestine (SJP)*. Available at: https://www.adl.org/resources/backgrounder/students-justice-palestine-sjp (Accessed: 21 December 2023).

32 Anti-Defamation League (2023a) *Anti-Israel Activism on U.S. Campuses, 2022-2023*. Available at: https://www.adl.org/resources/report/anti-israel-activism-us-campuses-2022-2023 (Accessed: 21 December 2023).

33 Vidino, L. (2023) *The Hamas Network in America*. Program on Extremism at George Washington. Available at: https://extremism.gwu.edu/sites/g/files/zaxdzs5746/files/2023-10/the-hamas-network-in-america.pdf (Accessed: 20 December 2023).

34 Baker, P. (2023) 'White House Disavows U.S. Islamic Group After Leader's Oct. 7 Remarks', *The New York Times*, 8 December.

35 Harvard CAPS, The Harris Poll and HarrisX (2023a) *Harvard CAPS Harris Poll December 2023*. Available at: https://harvardharrispoll.com/wp-content/uploads/2023/12/HHP_Dec23_Topline.pdf (Accessed: 21 December 2023); Harvard CAPS, The Harris Poll and HarrisX (2023b) *Harvard CAPS Harris Poll November 2023*. Available at: https://harvardharrispoll.com/wp-content/uploads/2023/11/HHP_Nov23_KeyResults.pdf (Accessed: 21 December 2023); Harvard CAPS, The Harris Poll and HarrisX (2023c) *Harvard CAPS Harris Poll October 2023*. Available at: https://t.co/GbeF9h39vt (Accessed: 21 December 2023).

36 Pew Research Center (2023) *Americans' Views of the Israel-Hamas War*. Available at: https://www.pewresearch.org/politics/2023/12/08/americans-views-of-the-israel-hamas-war/ (Accessed: 22 December 2023).

37 J Weisman, J., Igielnik, R. and McFadden, A. (2023) 'Poll Finds Wide Disapproval of Biden on Gaza, and Little Room to Shift Gears', *The New York Times*, 19 December. Available at: https://www.nytimes.com/2023/12/19/us/politics/biden-israel-gaza-poll.html (Accessed: 22 December 2023).

38 Hassner, R.E. (2023) 'From Which River to Which Sea?', *Wall Street Journal*, 5 December. Available at: https://www.wsj.com/articles/from-which-river-to-which-sea-anti-israel-protests-college-student-ignorance-a682463b (Accessed: 22 December 2023).

8 The Professors and the Pogrom

How the Theory of 'Zionist Settler Colonialism' Reframed the 7 October Massacre as 'Liberation'

Derek Spitz[1]

This chapter seeks to register and understand the deeper causes of the appalling reaction of parts of the western academic left to the massacre perpetrated by Hamas[2] on 7 October 2023. For the mask did not just slip. It was ripped off joyfully, ecstatically even, as if at the end of a masquerade. And what stood revealed was how far the decomposition has progressed, of a significant part of what passes itself off as the international left. First, let us review some examples from the miscellany, while recording, for us, the existential estrangement that trails in its wake.

Desublimating the Academy, or, What They Said

Joseph Massad, professor of Modern Arab Politics and Intellectual History at Columbia University, writing in *The Electronic Intifada* on the morning after the 7 October massacre, spoke of 'an innovative Palestinian resistance' in 'stunning videos' of Operation Al-Aqsa Flood. For him this was 'the Palestinian war of liberation.' Readers were invited to marvel, with Professor Massad, at the 'shocking success of the Palestinian offensive,' the 'major achievement of the resistance,' its takeover of several 'Israeli settler-colonies near the Gaza boundary and even as far away as 22kms, as in the case of Ofakim.' (Of course, these 'Israeli settler-colonies' are inside the recognised international borders of Israel proper. If *they* are 'settler colonies,' that tells you all you need to know about the popular favourite: 'from the river to the sea, etc.').[3]

Professor Massad's article shared exhilarated reports that thousands of Israelis 'were fleeing through the desert on foot … with many still hiding in settlements more than 24 hours into the resistance offensive.' Under the subheading of 'Jubilation and awe,' he wrote that 'The sight of the Palestinian resistance fighters storming Israeli checkpoints separating Gaza from Israel was astounding.' There were 'jubilant Arabs,' glued to the news, 'resistance

DOI: 10.4324/9781003497424-8

fighters' who 'marvelled at the rows of abandoned Israeli tanks.' For the author, apparently aflame with excitement, this was 'the stunning victory of the Palestinian resistance.'

Lake Micah, an Assistant Editor at *Harper's Magazine*, put it this way: 'to search for an analogue seems almost inappropriate to Palestinians' world historical (!) audacity to seize the components of self-determination for themselves.' Warming to his theme, he explained how 'the idiom of liberation invents itself anew with each instance that the yoke of bondage is sloughed off ... a near century's pulverized overtures toward ethnic realization, of groping for a medium of existential latitude –' before reaching his celebratory punchline: 'these things culminate in drastic actions in need of no apologia, the thrum of history as it develops is one of force; its inertia and advance require some momentum.'[4]

The prose is clotted, the rhythm onanistic, but the sentiment is clear: there are no, nor should there be any, limits on the glorious, ecstatic violence of the oppressed; they are on a world-historical mission.

Then there is Cornell University Professor of History, Russell Rickford. Addressing a rally at Cornell on 15 October, that is more than a week after the massacre was carried out, Rickford said of the Hamas pogrom that 'It was exhilarating. It was energizing' and that 'Palestinians of conscience' were 'able to breathe for the first time in years.' 'And if they weren't exhilarated by this challenge to the monopoly of violence, by this shifting of the balance of power, then they would not be human. *I was exhilarated.*'[5] (emphasis added)

A few days later, realising perhaps that not everyone felt similarly exhilarated by the torture, rape, beheading, butchering, burning, slaughter, and mass murder of grandmothers, grandfathers, men, women, children, babies, whole communities, entire generations, Jews, Arabs, Bedouin, and Thai, Professor Rickford thought better of it all, or at least of how he had *said* it all: 'I recognize that some of the language I used was reprehensible and did not reflect my values.' One need not parse the apology in any detail to notice how Rickford attributes the moral collapse of the enunciator to the infelicities of enunciation, rather than to his values, which he cordons off, to preserve unimplicated. He recapitulates this process of splitting-off more than once: 'I apologize for the horrible choice of words that I used in a portion of a speech that was intended to stress grassroots African American, Jewish and Palestinian traditions of resistance to oppression.' A few mischosen words, much to be regretted. The sentiment behind them, he can assure us, is entirely noble. However, Professor Rickford does not really say *which* African American or Jewish traditions of resistance to oppression he has in mind, that supposedly draw exhilaration from mass murder, in quite the way he did.

More than 24 hours after the pogrom, on 8 October, when sufficient details about its scope and character were already plainly available, Professor Gilbert

Achcar in the Department of Development Studies at SOAS blogged that the 'amazing and highly daring' 'counter-offensive (sic) launched by Hamas' was 'a much more spectacular feat' than the October 1973 war.[6] Going full supersessionist (and apparently unburdened by the international humanitarian law principle of distinction), Professor Achcar rhapsodised that it 'evokes the boldness of the biblical David in his fight against the giant Goliath,' that Hamas 'fighters' 'executed an amazing and highly daring offensive ...,' and that 'it is not difficult to understand the "enough-is-enough" logic behind Hamas' counter-offensive (sic).' Professor Achcar did go on to criticise Hamas from a tactical and perhaps even a strategic point of view (although not, mind you, from a moral point of view) by pointing out that the belief Hamas could achieve victory through intimate mass murder was 'magical thinking': the stuff, as it were, of dreams.

Professor Ashok Kumar, senior lecturer in Political Economy at Birkbeck, posted the following on Twitter/X (since deleted, and false in every one of its particulars): 'Sometimes partying on stolen land next to a concentration camp where a million people are starved has consequences.'[7]

Dr Shahd Hammouri, lecturer in law at Kent Law School, wrote that 'Resistance by the Palestinian people by all means available at their disposal against an illegal occupying power is a legitimate act.'[8]

Other professors have screamed 'Go Back to Poland!'[9] at Jews, torn down posters about the hostages of Hamas,[10] and even assaulted Jews.

Social Media Beside Itself

While this chapter focuses on the intellectual and moral collapse of a significant part of the international *academic* left, it is worth noting that social media was also quite beside itself, awash with elation. Thus, we were told that 'decolonisation is not a metaphor'; that 'today should be a day of celebration for supporters of democracy and human rights, as Gazans break out of their open-air prison and Hamas fighters cross into their colonisers' territory. The struggle for freedom is rarely bloodless and we shouldn't apologise for it'; that 'we are full of pride ... we are really really full of joy of [sic] what has happened'; and that 'You have to go away from here and go, this was just the start for you here. When we hear the resistance, the al Aqsa Flood, we must turn that flood into a tsunami over the whole world.' 'What,' we were asked, 'did y'all think decolonisation meant ... vibes? papers? essays? losers.'

In one striking instance of moral narcissism, dressed up as anti-racist indignation, we saw a performative radicalism that found it 'sickening' and 'a bit racist,' *not* that Hamas had just perpetrated a massacre, mostly of Jewish people, all living within the internationally recognised borders of the State of Israel, *but instead*, that some would presume to describe the massacre (perfectly accurately, as it happens) as a pogrom.

All of which brings to mind Walter Benjamin's observation in the last lines of the epilogue to *The Work of Art in the Age of Mechanical Reproduction*[11] that fascism tends towards the aestheticisation of politics. Welcome to the grim theatre of *Linksfaschismus*.

When Did Pogroms Go Progressive?

Leon Trotsky, in his classic *1905*, described the world-destroying absence of limit in the unfolding of an Eastern European pogrom:

> The doss-house tramp is king. A trembling slave an hour ago, hounded by police and starvation, he now feels himself an unlimited despot. Everything is allowed to him, he is capable of anything, he is the master of property and honour, of life and death. If he wants to, he can throw an old woman out of a third-floor window together with a grand piano, he can smash a chair against a baby's head, rape a little girl while the entire crowd looks on, hammer a nail into a living human body .... He exterminates whole families, he pours petrol over a house, transforms it into a mass of flames, and if anyone attempts to escape he finishes him off with a cudgel. A savage horde comes tearing into an Armenian almshouse, knifing old people, sick people, women, children .... There exist no tortures, figments of a feverish brain maddened by alcohol and fury, at which he need ever stop. He is capable of anything, he dares everything. God save the Tsar![12]

Suzan Quitaz has described the unbearable footage of the 7 October massacre, which was shown to international journalists to try to combat the rapid and perverse growth of efforts to minimise or deny the pogrom. Quitaz wrote in *Fathom*:[13]

> In the video, terrorists were shouting in Arabic with a Palestinian accent, they looked content and proud as they committed sadistic atrocities. They were talking among themselves saying 'I swear to Allah, I just killed the coward Jew dog who was hiding under the table.' That 'jew dog' was a young girl who was seen alive in the video hiding under [a] table-desk. They shot her at close range. Throughout the video words such as 'Allahu Akbar', meaning God is great, 'shot', 'give me a knife' and 'pray to Allah to bless me with another Jew dog to kill' were heard. We saw homes soaked in blood, we saw beheaded people, people slaughtered with knives, young women who had been raped, and people burned beyond recognition. We saw CCTV footage of terrorists standing on roadways in southern Israel shooting at civilian

cars as they speed away in fear. A car stops, terrorists surround it and continue shooting at close-range even when it's clear the occupants are already dead.

So how did parts of the academic left reframe the worst antisemitic pogrom since the Holocaust as 'resistance' and 'liberation'? In part it is because a large part of the academic left, taking up residence in the flatlands, now views the Israeli-Palestinian conflict through the lens of 'settler colonial studies' and the entire history of the Zionist movement and the Jewish State as 'Zionist Settler Colonialism.'[14] This paradigm divides the world into a crude and unbridgeable binary of colonisers and the colonised, oppressor and oppressed, 'whites' and 'people of colour'. It presents itself as a form of 'engaged' scholarship, but settler colonial studies also reframes and embraces a very particular form of violence – the kind of violence Hamas perpetrated on 7 October, pogromist violence without limit or restraint.

The Left's Fanonite Detour

Frantz Fanon occupies a position at the intellectual heart of settler colonial studies. He is celebrated today as an inspiration and founder of the research programme. But Fanon had a particular fascination with violence, seeing it as a cleansing act of self-constitution, a redemptive act of regeneration. This fascination echoes through his book, *The Wretched of the Earth.*[15] The first chapter, 'Concerning Violence,' is a paean to the therapeutic effects of violence for the colonial subject. Even if it is necessary to contextualise Fanon's treatment of revolutionary violence within the specific historical context of the armed struggle of the FLN in Algeria,[16] nevertheless, there remains an irreducible core that both advocates and justifies violence, attributing to it cathartic and self-actualising attributes for the colonial subject.[17]

National liberation, wrote Fanon 'is always a violent phenomenon .... Decolonization ... cannot come as a result of ... a friendly understanding .... The naked truth of decolonization evokes for us the searing bullets and bloodstained knives which emanate from it.' He continued, 'For if the last shall be first, this will only come to pass after a murderous and decisive struggle between the two protagonists .... From birth it is clear ... that this narrow world, strewn with prohibitions, can only be called into question by absolute violence.'[18]

For Fanon, the zones of coloniser and colonised were delineated as a stark binary: 'follow the principle of reciprocal exclusivity' he advised. 'No conciliation is possible, for of the two terms, one is superfluous....'[19] He gave violence a *constitutive* role: 'For the colonized people this violence, because it constitutes their only work, invests their characters with positive and creative qualities.'[20] It becomes a path to freedom: 'The colonized man finds his freedom in and through violence.'[21] Ultimately, for Fanon, 'violence is a cleansing force.'[22]

Fanon affirms the way in which 'The violence which has ruled over the ordering of the colonial world ... that same violence will be claimed and taken over by the native.' This happens 'at the moment when, deciding to embody history in his own person, he surges into the forbidden quarters.' And for the avoidance of doubt, 'The destruction of the colonial world is no more and no less than the abolition of one zone, its burial in the depths of the earth or its expulsion from the country.'[23] Fanon goes on: 'The native's challenge to the colonial world is not a rational confrontation of points of view. It is not a treatise on the universal....'[24]

For present purposes, I put to one side the fact that, as Simon Sebag Montefiore has correctly explained, when it comes to Israel/Palestine, 'the decolonisation narrative is dangerous and false,' 'does not accurately describe either the foundation of Israel or the tragedy of the Palestinians,' and 'is long overdue for serious challenge.'[25] That is plainly so, but my point is a narrower one. For Fanon, the exhortation to violence accompanying decolonisation, *and the violence itself* are, in the words of social theorist Moishe Postone, 'regarded ... per se as inherently emancipatory.'[26]

Compare Fanon's praise poem to the violence of the colonised with the Hamas Covenant 1988, the preamble to which contains the following pithy observations: 'Israel will exist and will continue to exist until Islam will obliterate it, just as it obliterated others before it'; and 'Our struggle against the Jews is very great and very serious. It needs all sincere efforts.' And then to the infamous but still under-reported Article 7 of the Covenant: 'The Day of Judgement will not come about until Moslems fight the Jews (killing the Jews), when the Jew will hide behind stones and trees. The stones and trees will say O Moslems, O Abdulla, there is a Jew behind me, come and kill him.' And Article 15: 'In face of the Jews' usurpation of Palestine, it is compulsory that the banner of Jihad be raised.'[27]

The South African Alternative

Back in the days when the decent left was still a majority, it used to say that the organisational forms adopted during the course of a struggle prefigured the institutional forms that leftists hoped to build after that struggle had succeeded. Democratic modes of struggle offered a seedbed for the democratic institutions it was hoped would then grow and bear fruit. The old left grounding in social democratic theory, universalist forms of analysis, and enlightenment principles led to a very different attitude to violence.

Consider the example of the democratic organs of working-class power, concentrated in the independent non-racial trade union movement in South

Africa, first in the Federation of South African Trade Unions (FOSATU) and then in its successor, the Congress of South African Trade Unions (COSATU). Those workshops of shop floor democracy were the laboratories in which militant but measured trade unionism took advantage of a newly minted legal right to strike and developed the 'unfair labour practice' jurisprudence, as one instance of an embryonic culture based on the rule of law. The new South African Constitution, one of the most progressive anywhere, was decidedly not born of a project that celebrates the violence of the colonised as intrinsic and therapeutic. The constitutional guarantees to hold executive power to account and protect minority rights are an achievement to be celebrated as an entrenchment of the rule of law. That is the sort of thing the decent left used to care deeply about. Homegrown trade union power, for example, was one of the preconditions for and cornerstones of constitutional democracy. But that power looks nothing like Fanon's 'searing bullets and bloodstained knives' nor the rapture of his 'engaged' acolytes.

Nor should 'the oppressed' be treated as if they lacked all agency. Even in the face of material constraints on the scope of that agency, there are always choices to be made. Consider, again, the South African resistance movement. It was never a principle or policy of the ANC's armed struggle in South Africa to attack and randomly murder South African civilians. It was never tempted by the depravities of Hamas.

The form of violence adopted by the ANC in December 1961 was 'to launch a campaign of non-lethal sabotage.'[28] Even that campaign of sabotage was the subject of 'significant contemporary opposition' from within the ANC.[29] Moreover, in 1980, the ANC signed a declaration of adherence to the Geneva Conventions of 1949 and Protocol 1 of 1977, which states that 'parties to the conflict shall at all times distinguish between the civilian population and combatants.'[30] This was an 'almost unprecedented action by a liberation movement.'[31]

During the Rivonia Trial for founding the ANC's military wing, uMkhonto we Sizwe (the Spear of the Nation) or MK, Nelson Mandela explained the specific and unusual form taken by the ANC's 'turn to violence' by reference to the need to 'canalise and control' violence to avoid 'outbreaks of terrorism which would produce an intensity of bitterness and hostility between the various races of the country which is not produced even by war.'[32]

In June 1961, Mandela's arguments on armed struggle presented to the Joint Executives of the Congress Alliance were concerned with the need to *pre-empt and prevent* indiscriminate terrorism (precisely the thing now *exalted* by a significant part of the academic left). As Mandela put it:

> Look, this thing has already started in our country …. Let us take the same decision and lead. Because otherwise it will just deteriorate into a terrorist movement …. And if it's a terrorist organisation it's going to lead to the slaughter of human beings. Let us enter and lead.[33]

The ANC's 'commitment to avoiding extensive violence against civilians' is striking.[34] This sensibility was deeply embedded organisationally and it was more than merely a matter of tactics. It had something to do with an implicit commitment to a universal political morality, and an explicit awareness that indiscriminate violence against civilians 'would also have a terrible human cost and threaten post-apartheid reconstruction.'[35]

To repeat: it was never a principle or policy of the ANC in South Africa to attack and randomly murder South African civilians. The same cannot be said of many of the forms of Palestinian struggle. To ignore the starkness of this *qualitative* difference is surely to indulge in the racism of low expectations. The oppressed have agency. They are moral human beings. They only live in an iron-clad world of 'no options' if they have first been turned into metaphors, made into the bearers of western projections; in short, Orientalised.

Conclusion: Violence and Politics

The social theorist Moishe Postone has elaborated on the connection between forms of violence and forms of politics:

> I would like to suggest that there is a fundamental difference between movements that do not target civilians randomly (such as the Viet Minh and Viet Cong and the ANC) and those that do (such as the IRA, al-Qaeda, and Hamas). This difference is not simply tactical but profoundly political; a relation exists between the form of violence and the form of politics. That is, I want to suggest that the sort of future society and polity implicitly expressed by the political praxis of militant social movements that distinguish military from civilian targets differs from that implied by the praxis of movements that make no such distinction. The latter tend to be concerned with identity. In the broadest sense they are radically nationalist, *operating on the basis of a friend/foe distinction that essentializes a civilian population as the enemy and closes off the possibility of future coexistence.* For that reason, the programs of such movements present little in the way of socioeconomic analysis aimed at transforming social structures (which should not be conflated with social services, which movements may or may not provide).[36] (emphasis added)

The second intifada, which began in September 2000, involved setting off bombs, frequently suicide bombs, on buses, in pizza parlours, discotheques, and Passover Seders. It was a devastating blow to the Israeli left, from which it has not recovered. It is already obvious that the Hamas pogrom on 7 October sounds the death-knell for the fantasy of a 'one-state solution.' If its invocation was always fantastical, after 7 October it has become morally grotesque. For the Hamas pogrom asks and answers the question whether the principal grievance 'is not the absence of a desired nation-state but the existence of another one.'[37] In any event, the ramifications of that day are also, or at least should be, far-reaching for the academic left's research programme of settler colonial studies. Its reaction to the Hamas pogrom announces that paradigm's degeneration.

Notes

1 An earlier version of this chapter first appeared in *Fathom*, on November 28, 2023, https://fathomjournal.org/universities-in-crisis-the-professors-and-the-pogrom. It is reproduced with the kind permission of the editor.
2 Uncannily, the Hebrew Bible mentions the word 'hamas' early, in Genesis 6:11: 'And the earth was corrupt before God and the earth was filled with outrage.' The word 'outrage' is also translated as 'violence' or as a couple: 'violent outrage.' And the Hebrew word for violence as outrage is 'hamas.' In the Midrashic commentaries, Breishit Rabba 31:6, the Hebrew word for violence and murder, for complete moral destruction, is 'hamas': '...Hamas refers to idolatry; hamas refers to sexual immorality; hamas refers to bloodshed.' Of course, the Hebrew word is not the Arabic acronym for the 'Islamic' 'Resistance' 'Movement' (Hamas). Nevertheless, it is as if a haunting were to enter the domain of prophecy, i.e. the uncanny.
3 electronicintifada.net/content/just-another-battle-or-palestinian-war-liberation/38661
4 twitter.com/afrofatalism/status/1710859449605230697
5 cornellsun.com/2023/10/16/cornell-professor-exhilerated-by-hamass-attack-defends-remark/
6 gilbert-achcar.net/on-hamas-counter-offensive
7 thetimes.co.uk/article/Israel-palestine-uk-academics-ucl-oxford-cambridge
8 law4palestine.org/the-palestinian-people-have-the-right-to-resistance-by-all-means-available-at-their-disposal-dr-shahd-hammouri/
9 https://www.jpost.com/diaspora/antisemitism/article-772592
10 fathomjournal.org/progressives-and-the-hamas-pogrom-an-a-z-guide/
11 (London: Penguin Books, 2008).
12 Trotsky, L. (2016) *1905*. Chicago: Haymarket Books, p. 113.
13 fathomjournal.org/daddy-daddy-god-why-am-i-alive-a-harrowing-report-from-a-journalist-who-watched-raw-footage-of-the-hamas-pogrom-of-7-october/
14 See Johnson, A. (2021) 'Can't You See He's Fooled You All? An Open Letter to Peter Gabriel et al Explaining Why Israel Is not a "Settler Colonial State",' *Fathom*, November 2021.
15 Fanon, F. (2001) *The Wretched of the Earth*. London: Penguin Books, pp. 27–84.
16 Macey, D. (2012) *Frantz Fanon: A Biography*. London: Verso, pp. 450–451; 470–471, 473: 'In Algeria violence was not just the midwife of history. Violence was Algeria's father and mother.'
17 For a powerful encapsulation of Fanon's thinking in *The Wretched of the Earth*, see Silverman, M (2009) 'Frantz Fanon: Colonialism and Violence,' *Postcolonial Thought in the French Speaking World*, ed. Charles Forsdick and David Murphy. Liverpool: Liverpool University Press, pp. 83–84.

18 Fanon, *The Wretched of the Earth*, 27–29.
19 Ibid., 31.
20 Ibid., 73.
21 Ibid., 67–68.
22 Ibid., 74.
23 Ibid., 31.
24 Ibid., 31.
25 Sebag Montefiore, S. (2023) 'The Decolonization Narrative Is Dangerous and False,' *The Atlantic*, October 27, 2023, pp. 1, 2, 5, 8.
26 See Postone, M (2006) 'History and Helplessness: Mass Mobilization and Contemporary Forms of Anticapitalism,' *Public Culture* 18, no. 1, pp. 106–107 for a compelling critique of this notion.
27 Avalon.law.yale.edu/20th_century/hamas.asp
28 Stevens, S. (2019) 'The Turn to Sabotage by the Congress Movement in South Africa,' *Past and Present*, 245, no. 1, p. 225.
29 Ibid., 223. The available evidence shows 'that both before and after the "turn to sabotage", the determining factor in Congress leaders' attitudes towards the use of violent means was their fear of the social and political consequences of popular enthusiasm for violence and of the possibility that such popular enthusiasm might lead to violence becoming indiscriminate. Once the decision to "turn to violence" had been made, the same fear also determined the form of the violent activities that were undertaken by MK' (ibid., 227). Throughout the 1950s, 'Congress leaders not only resisted pressure from below for the Congress movement itself to initiate or prepare for violent action. They also declined to sanction or facilitate violent activity by supporters. ... [They] condemned and sought to suppress the unsanctioned violent activity that nonetheless occurred' (ibid., 231). 'The Congress leadership was haunted by the "fear that action by their supporters could spiral out of their control into indiscriminate and/or racialized violence..."Mau-Mau tactics", associated with the indiscriminate violence against African "loyalists" and white settlers, were to be condemned and discouraged, not replicated' (ibid., 234). The distance between this and the form of violence that undergirds the academic paradigm of settler colonial studies is vast.
30 Statement on Signing Declaration on behalf of the ANC and Umkhonto We Sizwe, Adhering to the Geneva Conventions of 1949 and Protocol 1 of 1977, at the Headquarters of the International Committee of the Red Cross, Geneva, November 28, 1980, https:omalley.nelsonmandela.org/omally/cis/omalley/OmalleyWeb/031v024 24/041v02730/05lv02918/061v02979.htm.
31 Cherry, J. (2000) 'Just War and Just Means: Was the TRC Wrong about the ANC?', *Transformation* 42, p. 19.
32 Mandela, N. 'I Am Prepared to Die,' cited in Stevens, 'The Turn to Sabotage,' p. 226.
33 'Mandela-Stengel Conversations: Transcripts of the Audio Recordings of Conversations in 1992 and 1993 between Nelson Mandela and Richard Stengel during the making of *Long Walk to Freedom*,' 620, unpublished document, Nelson Mandela Foundation, Johannesburg, cited in Stevens, 'The Turn to Sabotage,' p. 238.
34 Stevens, 'The Turn to Sabotage,' p. 255.
35 Ibid., 240. There were terrible occasions when civilians were killed during the attacks. Indeed, the Truth and Reconciliation Commission said that 'Whilst it recognised that it was ANC policy that the loss of civilian life should be "avoided", there were instances where members of MK perpetrated gross violations of human rights

in that the distinction between military and civilian targets was blurred in certain armed actions … resulting in gross violations of human rights through civilian injury and loss of life.' TRC Report, vol. 5, chapter 6, 'Findings and Conclusions: Violations Committed in the Course of the Armed Struggle,' paragraph 136, https://web.stanford.edu/class/history48q/assets/files/documents/EMBARGO/5chap6.htm.

36 Postone, 'History and Helplessness,' p. 105.

37 Mor, S. (2023) 'Ecstasy and Amnesia in the Gaza Strip,' *Mosaic Magazine*, November 6, 2023, mosaicmagazine.com/essay/Israel-zionism/2023/11/ecstasy-and-amnesia-in-the-gaza-strip/.

9 October 7 and the Antisemitic War of Words

Cary Nelson

There are no adequate words. Nouns and adjectives alike die on the tongue before they are spoken. Appalling, barbaric, bestial, criminal, demonic, despicable, evil, grisly, horrific, immoral, inhuman, insane, merciless, monstrous, obscene, savage, uncivilized, unspeakable. The substitutions continue, even within the same document, but the goal of the proper, sufficient designation cannot be reached. The need to find a form of condemnation that matches the level of violence on October 7 is necessarily in tension with awareness that the hate-driven particulars of the violence remain essentially incomprehensible. Not political passion nor indoctrination, not training nor planning, not medication nor group solidarity, not even deeply internalized hatred can fully explain the conduct of the massacre. To speak about the actions visible in videos, to narrate reconstructed sequences of events, to detail particular Hamas assaults, all these attempts to testify after the fact feel like they betray the fundamental character of what was done. The raw pain of survivors holds as much authenticity of witness as one might ask for, but even then the mediation language imposes often limits us to empathy, putting both representation and understanding beyond reach.

In this the most serious mass murder of Jews since the Holocaust—despite the vast difference in scale, duration, and historical context—some uncanny parallels obtain. There is the duality of organized general planning and opportunistic malicious execution by individuals. Individual Nazi SS troops and Hamas terrorists frequently had all the latitude they needed to personalize the killings they carried out. Both sometimes took glee in butchering babies by hand. Neither spared men, women, children, or the elderly. Contempt for their victims had not only to be felt but also expressed and celebrated, to be commemorated indelibly. Antisemitism of course was motive and overt rationale. There was no shame remaining in the designation.

It is nearly impossible to endure thinking about these events—either to dwell on what actually took place in the towns and kibbutzim near the border or to contemplate the consequent losses in suffering or public security. Yet Israelis and those who lost friends or family to death or capture have little choice. They cannot long find relief from the burden of reality. The thousands

DOI: 10.4324/9781003497424-9

called up for military service have no choice. They are at war in practice and within war. Psychologically. Two million Gazans have no choice as they face frequently impossible living conditions and choices every day. The alternative for some Jews is to find something to do, whether volunteering to help the Israeli harvest or, less meaningfully, writing a short essay like this. You stay occupied. Thinking alone is not helpful.

Meanwhile, the political war of position imposes further conditions of impossibility on Israel's response to the contemporary massacre. In a war of position as Antonio Gramsci conceived it, a cultural struggle unfolds gradually in search of conceptual and political dominance. In the resulting debates foundering on their antisemitic base, Israel's wartime options only register paralysis. Hurry up, please, it's time; you only have days or weeks to continue the military operation. But take infinite care; go slowly to protect innocent lives. Such contradictions remain uncontested in the press and from government spokespersons as the competing demands persist. The international community rapidly reached consensus: Israel has the right to defend itself, but there is no way that right can be justly exercised. It is only an abstraction. Condemn Hamas, then turn the other cheek. Defeat Hamas while instituting a ceasefire. Holding those two aims in view at the same time is either meaningless or thoroughly disabling. Yet that is what Israel was asked to do from the outset.

As with the Nazis, academic apologists for antisemitism once again have a special role to play in the war of position that aims to shape public debate about both the pogrom and Israel's response. I will focus on two continuing faculty interventions, those from former George Washington University psychology professor Lara Sheehi (at the Doha Institute of Graduate Studies in Qatar as of January 2024) and those from Brown University historian and Holocaust scholar professor Omer Bartov. Both have a history of anti-Zionism, though Bartov appears to be capable of pretending otherwise. Unlike Bartov, however, Sheehi has for several years explicitly embraced Hamas. Her hostility to Israel functions as a badge of honor. Sheehi aims to rationalize the Hamas assault, Bartov to discredit Israel's Gaza campaign.

On October 24, 2020, Lara Sheehi tweeted a characteristic declaration: 'FUCK ZIONISM, ZIONISTS, AND SETTLER COLONIALISM using Palestinian lives as examples of their boundless cruelty and power. Anyone who can't yet get it, peddles "both sides" BS and doesn't denounce this persistent violence is complicit.' On May 22, 2021, she tweeted, 'If you see this and STILL entertain for even a split second that Hamas is a terrorist entity, there is literally zero hope for you, your soul, or your general existence as an ethical human being in this world.'[1] In her essays, her coauthored book *Psychoanalysis Under Occupation*, and scores and scores of tweets over nearly a decade she stablished herself as a fierce and relentless anti-Zionist. In an October 27, 2023, video interview hosted by Jared Ware, Sheehi responded to Hamas's October 7 assault by declaring that 'We have to rid ourselves of the romantic notions of what uprisings look like.'[2] We need to interrogate her remark by asking what it actually means. Hamas's contempt for its victims is matched by Sheehi's contempt for those who do not agree with her about the necessity for radical violence as the only authentic form of resistance to settler colonialism. In the call for revolutionary violence, she regularly invokes Frantz Fanon. Of course there are alternatives, violent uprisings short of the gleeful butchery of October 7 and revolutions carried out substantially with nonviolent resistance. But Sheehi finds everything Hamas did on that day necessary and instructive, essential to the project of liberation. There is no excess to condemn, no violation of the norms that should govern revolutionary conduct. It was all just as it should be. Shame on us if we falter or show weakness in our resolve to embrace the events of the day. The effect is to justify not only infinite varieties of violence against Israelis but also an extraordinary escalation of terrorist violence overall.

For so many faculty and students in the West, the unacceptable details of the massacre are displaced by a celebratory chant: 'From the river to the sea, Palestine will be free.' The abstract, idealized goal of erasing the Jewish state absorbs the gruesome particulars of actually trying to carry out that aim. And the joyous camaraderie of group celebration cements the transformation. But not for Sheehi. All that is a romanticized form of denial. We must take the butchered babies in hand and hold them up to the light.

Sheehi at least deserves credit for her honesty, her frankness in going further into the darkness than other faculty who share her politics. She has no use for the useful idiots of many ages on campus who absolve one another of the responsibility to confront what actually happened. She scolds us for our deluded failure to embrace the quotidian necessities of revolution. Like Hamas itself, she embraces all that was done and sees it as a blueprint for what must be done again. Can she persuade others to adopt the violence as if it were their own? Some certainly, especially those who can be convinced to see it as a natural progression from where they already are. Others will tolerate only the sanitized celebration. Many in the West voice a moment's regret for Hamas's conduct, then quickly move on to denounce the violence of Israel's bombing campaign and ground invasion.

Omer Bartov, focusing his attention on Part II of the war of position, crafts a particularly clever condemnation of the ground invasion in his November 10 *New York Times* essay 'What I Believe as a Historian of Genocide.' He has also produced capsule televised versions of his argument on MSNBC, *Al Jazeera*, and elsewhere. Perhaps recognizing that the accusation that Israel is committing genocide in Gaza has lost much of its credibility through being repeated over several years of Gaza population growth and relatively limited numbers of wartime deaths, Bartov chooses a far more subtle strategy. Like Sheehi, he comes to the challenge with a personal history. In the summer of 2023, for example, he organized a group letter, 'The Elephant in the Room,' which was issued on August 4. It decries the purported Israeli effort to 'ethnically cleanse all territories under Israeli rule of their Palestinian population' as part of overall ideology of 'Jewish supremacism.'[3] Although the letter does not explicitly apply the claim to Israel within its pre-1967 borders, one cannot avoid the implication that the cleansing goal entails that intention as well. As a Holocaust scholar, moreover, Bartov knows that 'cleansing' Germany of its Jews was a favorite Nazi metaphor well before the Holocaust, one that helped prepare the public psychologically for the final solution.

His *New York Times* column opens by applying the charge of ethnic cleansing to Gaza and warning that 'it is crucial to warn of the potential for genocide before it occurs, rather than belatedly condemn it after it has taken place.' Indeed, taking on the mantle of a responsible historian, he urges us not to claim genocide is already under way in Gaza. Instead, he points out that 'Israeli leaders and generals have made terrifying pronouncements that indicate a genocidal intent' and adds 'there is genocidal intent, which can easily tip into genocidal action.' Predictably, the anti-Zionist left has taken Bartov's attribution of genocidal intent as gospel. He quotes Israeli political and military leaders apparently venting with anger and a desire for retribution from October 7-10, in the immediate aftermath of the October 7 pogrom.

Among Bartov's other examples is this key one: 'On Oct. 9, Israel's defense minister, Yoav Gallant, said, "We are fighting human animals and we are acting accordingly," a statement indicating dehumanization, which has genocidal echoes.' It represents 'rage- and vengeance-filled rhetoric that dehumanizes the population of Gaza and calls for its extinction.' People spoke in anguish in the wake of the pogrom. Unfortunately, Bartov relied on press reports of Gallant's remarks instead of examining the original Hebrew texts. In a detailed and carefully researched essay in *The Atlantic*, Yair Rosenberg documents and translates that what Gallant actually said in videotaped October 10 remarks was 'Gaza will not return to what it was before. There will be no Hamas. We will eliminate it all.'[4] Press reports claimed that Gallant had pledged to eliminate all of Gaza, which is clearly not the case. Gallant also makes the 'human animals' reference quite specific: 'We are fighting against human animals. This is the ISIS of Gaza.' Again, the reference is to Hamas as Gaza's version of ISIS, not to the entire Gazan population.

Nonetheless, extremist Israeli politicians did vent their rage. To pretend that the remarks by Gallant and others amount either to policy or potential escalation, however, is not merely unwarranted; it is irresponsible and irrational. It misrepresents Israel's national character, discounts the ethical constraints that govern IDF conduct, and ignores the political calculations that had already limited the actions Israelis were willing to take. Despite anguish more intense than anything Israelis have experienced in generations, the Israeli public would not tolerate actual genocide. Nor would the international community. Bartov's hypothetical warning of genocide in Gaza is both a moral and political slander. But for many on the radical left, the only difference between 'genocidal intent' and genocide is that Israel has not yet succeeded in eliminating the entire Gazan population.

Nonetheless, it is very clever, encouraging Israel's opponents to cry 'genocide' without actually claiming it is under way: 'functionally and rhetorically we may be watching an ethnic cleansing operation that could quickly devolve into genocide, as has happened more than once in the past.' As Bartov states in a November 10 *Democracy Now* interview, 'my own sense is that it is not genocide at the moment, because there is still no clear indication of an attempt to destroy the entire population, which would be genocide, but that we are very close on the verge of that.'[5] More than most of us, Bartov is aware he is alluding to the slander that Israelis are the new Nazis. 'More than once,' of course, technically invokes Rwanda and other examples, but there is really only one comparison with the power to stigmatize Israel, and that is Nazi Germany.

Bartov cements the comparison with Nazism that he seems to have neither the courage nor the candor to express directly by telling us there is a special constituency that should intervene: 'I urge such venerable institutions as the United States Holocaust Memorial Museum in Washington, D.C., and Yad Vashem in Jerusalem to step in now and stand at the forefront of those warning against war crimes, crimes against humanity, ethnic cleansing and the crime of all crimes, genocide.' He then broadens the appeal by suggesting that the most telling universal lessons of the Holocaust, the inhumanity of the murder of millions, are directly implicated in Israel's conduct in Gaza. Israelis are the new Nazis, and we are the indifferent accomplices if we fail to act: 'If we truly believe that the Holocaust taught us a lesson about the need—or really, the duty—to preserve our own humanity and dignity by protecting those of others, this is the time to stand up and raise our voices, before Israel's leadership plunges it and its neighbors into the abyss.' Bartov is no longer warning that Israel may slip unwittingly into genocide. That was already an unjustified fear and a manipulative political argument. Now he is telling us that is what Israel's political leadership wants and will try to get away with if we allow them. But 'There is still time to stop Israel from letting its actions become a genocide. We cannot wait a moment longer.'

There is slippage here between two political predictions: unintentional genocide and deliberate genocide. He shifts between them repeatedly to make the probability more convincing. But both are divorced from reality. We are not after all talking about millions of Israelis sweeping across Gaza in a murderous frenzy. We are talking about the Israeli Defense Forces. There is only one party to the conflict that dreams and acts that way: Hamas. Bartov has apparently discounted that fact. Does he really suppose the IDF could drift unwittingly into the slaughter of a million Gazans? Or, worse still, work out a plan to do so? Bartov is of course lending his prestige as a Holocaust scholar to contemporary political analysis, a field in which he does not have special expertise or authority.

Bartov also operates with indicative historical blinders. In a November 13 Zoom presentation co-organized by the decisively anti-Zionist *Jewish Currents*, he objected to characterizing October 7 as a pogrom because a pogrom is an attack on a minority, and Jews are not a minority in the state of Israel.[6] Of course, as he well knows, Jews are a minority in the region, surrounded by Arab states. He also insisted that the Hamas assault could not be considered part of the long history of Jewish persecution, a bizarre claim given that Arab antisemitism, as Bartov also well knows, was substantially informed by Nazi World War II propaganda.

Bartov apparently wants to trade on his expertise as a Holocaust scholar to convince us he is qualified to ask whether conditions are ripe for another genocide to emerge. Hence the title of his essay, 'What I Believe as a Historian of Genocide.'[7] He can certainly speculate, and some will surely find him credible. The problem for Bartov is that conditions are *not* ripe for Israel to commit genocide. He is unfortunately not the only Holocaust scholar to succumb to the lure of Holocaust inversion. A clear-headed analysis makes it apparent that an actual Israeli-led genocide is not possible. If Hamas had the requisite power, genocide against Israelis would unfold rapidly. If Hezbollah and Iran joined with Hamas, the existential threat to Israel would be definitive. That remains the only threat of genocide overhanging the Middle East.

There is a still more credible threat built into both Sheehi's and Bartov's project: the increasing challenge to Israel's legitimacy. Sheehi would have us believe Hamas, not Israel, is the one engaged in a just war. If it is a crime against humanity, it is a necessary one. Bartov simply wants to persuade us Israel's war is morally unjustified, itself a crime against humanity. Although their arguments are distinctive—and are of interest because of that—they also represent the two overall anti-Zionist approaches in the current war of position, one focused on the Hamas pogrom, the other on Israel's invasion. Sheehi aims for legitimation, Bartov for delegitimization. That comprises two sides of the same coin. They both aim to shift the weight of international moral judgment.

Does that matter? Unfortunately, it does. We are being flooded with letters, op-eds, and essays aimed at shaping both public opinion and public policy about the war with Hamas. Sheehi and Bartov both have followers in the academy they evidently hope to influence. Moreover, they are simultaneously empowering and speaking for the international anti-Zionist left. And both have used online media to reach the broader public. No one believes Israel can sustain a viable future without some level of international support. The war of position is a war for the balance of power on that front. If Hamas is not defeated, it will be back. Perhaps the issue will be resolved before this chapter appears in print.

Meanwhile, what we know with certainty is that the war of position has escalated. Even if it abates in time when the current war ends, it will have established a new floor, a new higher minimum level of continuing anti-Zionist and antisemitic hostility. The new normal for antizionist rhetoric will be rhetoric saturated with hate. One place that outcome is guaranteed is on campus, where anti-Zionist faculty activism, scholarship, and teaching already dominated the humanities and interpretive social sciences. Some of those disciplines will now do exclusively anti-Zionist faculty hiring and student recruitment. A number of the constituent disciplines will be thoroughly hostile environments for Jewish students. And they will graduate students more hostile to Israel, who will carry those views with them into many professions. We need to do everything we can to combat those trends. But nothing short of a two-state resolution to the Israeli-Palestinian conflict can dislodge increasing anti-Zionism in the academy of the West.

Notes

1 See Nelson, C. (2023) 'Lara Sheehi's Joyous Rage: Antisemitic Anti-Zionism, Advocacy Academia and Jewish Students' Nightmares at GWU' for documentation of these and other online posts. *Fathom*. April 2023. Available at: https://fathomjournal.org/lara-sheehis-joyous-rage-antisemitic-anti-zionism-advocacy-academia-and-jewish-students-nightmares-at-gwu/.

2 Sheehi, L. (2023) 'Against Alienation—Lara Sheehi and Stephen Sheehi on their book *Psychoanalysis under Occupation: Practicing Resistance in Palestine*,' *Millennials Are Killing Capitalism*. 27 October, 2023. Available at: https://ww w.youtube.com/watch?v=duZfw-CGEZk.

3 Bartov, O et al (2022) 'The Elephant in the Room,' *Portside*. 6 August 2023. Available at: https://portside.org/2023-08-06/elephant-room.

4 Rosenberg, Y. (2024) 'What Did Top Israeli War Officials Really Say About Gaza?' *The Atlantic*. 21 January. Available at: https://www.theatlantic.com/international/archive/2024/01/israel-south-africa-genocide-case-fake-quotes/677198/.

5 Democracy Now. (2023) '"Clear Intention of Ethnic Cleansing": Israeli Holocaust Scholar Omer Bartov Warns of Genocide in Gaza'. 10 November 2023. Available at: https://www.democracynow.org/2023/11/10/bartov_genocide_apartheid.

6 Jewish Currents. (2023). 'Hijacking Memory: The Holocaust and the Siege of Gaza'. 13 November 2023. Available at: https://jewishcurrents.org/event/hijacking-memory-the-holocaust-and-the-siege-of-gaza.

7 Bartov, O. (2023) 'What I Believe as a Historian of Genocide', *New York Times*. 10 November 2023. Available at: https://www.nytimes.com/2023/11/10/opinion/israel-gaza-genocide-war.html.

10 Ancient Historians Embrace Debunked Conspiracy Theories Denying that Jews Are Indigenous to Israel

Brett Kaufman

In an attempt to defend the Hamas terrorist atrocities of October 7, 2023 as legitimate acts of resistance, a group of classicists, ancient historians, and archaeologists at elite American and international universities have claimed that Jews have no ancestral connection to the Land of Israel. The fact that they deny the very existence of one of the most well-documented ancient cultures in order to push a political agenda strikes a devastating blow to the integrity of the humanities. The alignment of inscriptions, artifacts, material culture, and historical texts that range from showing the life of everyday Israelites to striking historical documentation of biblical events and major figures in Jewish history attests to the antiquity of Jews in their Levantine homeland over a period of three millennia.

At issue is an open letter[1] circulating since October 20, 2023 to the time of writing entitled 'Letter of Solidarity with the people of Palestine,' wherein my colleagues commit themselves to a polemic that includes several misleading, non-factual, and ahistorical pronouncements. For example, they call the establishment of the State of Israel in 1948 'unlawful,' ignoring that the Jewish state was sanctioned by the historic 1947 United Nations General Assembly vote on Resolution 181 (II). Where they would expect to find stronger legal authenticity than that is puzzling. They place the blame for the current Gaza war and unfolding human tragedy squarely on Israel, without mentioning the Hamas-led murder, rape, torture, decapitation, and burning of around 1,200 people as well as the abduction of over 250 hostages from a multitude of countries on October 7, the vast majority of them unarmed civilians, or Hamas's use of Gazan civilians as human shields.[2] They would call this a 'biased' or 'decontextualized' approach to data for any other case study. Whereas United States officials have praised Israel's self-defense strategy as exceeding moral standards in the protection of noncombatant lives,[3] and whereas even official Palestinian statistics estimate a tenfold population increase since 1948,[4] my colleagues call it 'genocide.'

But the sentence that stands out the most, given the signatories' purported fields of expertise, is the following: 'We further renounce the use of the methods of our fields, especially archeological practices, by Zionist movements

DOI: 10.4324/9781003497424-10

which attempt to falsify a historical claim to the land by laundering its antiquity.' In other words, the signatories assert that Jews have no ancient or historic connection to the Land of Israel and intimate that Zionist (here a dog whistle for 'Jewish') archaeologists have faked any data that would prove it.

But they are mistaken. Saying Jews are indigenous to Israel is like saying Athenians are indigenous to Greece and Romans came from Italy. This is objectively uncontroversial.

At the City of David archaeological site in Jerusalem, where I research the metal weapons, tools, and scrap from the earliest Israelite palace dated to around 1000 BC, my late colleague Eilat Mazar discovered artifacts that proved the structure was the royal residence of ancient Judah.

She excavated Paleo-Hebrew inscriptions naming scribes, for example 'Yehuchal son of Shelmiyahu son of Shavi,' who is mentioned twice in the Old Testament Book of Jeremiah as a high official in the early 6th century BC court of Judean King Zedekiah.[5]

King David himself is mentioned in a 9th century BC inscription known as the Tel Dan stele, where an Aramaean victor recounts defeating a 'king of Israel' and 'the House of David.'[6]

Neo-Assyrian emperor Sennacherib commissioned an inscription following his failed 701 BC attempt to sack Jerusalem, in which he boasts of trapping biblical king 'Hezekiah the Jew ... in Jerusalem, his royal residence.'[7] The Mesopotamian annals of the aborted siege mirror the biblical accounts of Isaiah, II Kings, and Chronicles. Such raids by the Neo-Assyrians and later Neo-Babylonian king Nebuchadnezzar II (also archaeologically, historically, and epigraphically verified) led to widespread displacement of the Israelites, and is how Jewish diaspora communities came to exist in Iran, Iraq, Kurdistan, and other places across the Middle East and North Africa.[8,9]

Roman emperor Titus celebrated his AD 70 sacking of Jerusalem and the destruction of the Israelites' Second Temple by depicting Roman soldiers carrying off the sacred menorah.[10] You can still see them today on his triumphal arch in the Forum of Rome. Jewish slaves transported to Rome by Titus is how many Jews wound up in Europe.

Hebrew, the Jewish national tongue, is an Iron Age evolution of Bronze Age Canaanite, both part of the Northwest Semitic family of languages indigenous to the Levant. Its use as a liturgical or spoken language has gone uninterrupted for over 3,000 years.[11] The Dead Sea Scrolls document the evolution of ancient Jewish religious practice and the Hebrew Bible.[12]

In Surahs al-Ma'idah 5:20-21 and al-Isra 17:104, Early Muslim writers of the Koran insisted that the 'Holy Land' is promised to the 'children of Israel' and 'the people of Moses'.

These are just a few examples of what my colleagues shockingly refer to as a 'false historical narrative.'

Although there is a tendency for non-specialists to read the Hebrew Bible or Old Testament as a series of invented stories and popular myths or as purely a religious document, there is an overwhelming record of historical, archaeological, and genetic data collected over the past century and a half confirming the indigeneity of Jews to Israel.[13] Generations of renowned biblical archaeologists and Semitic philologists have published extensively on the artifacts, inscriptions, and textual evidence.[14]

Anyone who has taken the time to familiarize themselves with the work of these scholars would find that the evidence for Jewish ancestry in ancient Israel is incontrovertible. This evidence helps make sense of why exiled Jews in the diaspora have longed continually for their homeland over the past two millennia since expulsion by the Romans. But somehow, this large group of faculty and student signatories who are supposed to be specialists of Mediterranean antiquity are not convinced.

My colleagues join an age-old tradition of attempts to write the Jews out of history. Aryan ideologues of the 19th century tried to erase ancient Northwest Semitic contributions to Western civilization, particularly those of the Phoenicians (because of their close relationship with the Israelites) to Classical Greece, contradicting the ancient Greek writers themselves. The historical fact of Phoenician involvement in Greece was inconvenient to the Aryan search for white European eugenic and intellectual purity. Modern scholars have debunked such pseudo-scholarship, from Cyrus H. Gordon[15] to Michael Astour[16] to Martin Bernal[17] to Sarah Morris[18] to Walter Burkert[19] to Carolina López-Ruiz.[20] As Bernal[21] has shown, in this context anti-Phoenicianism was thinly veiled antisemitism.

In recent decades, however, outright erasure of the Israelites themselves has gained steam and has come to be known by the benign-sounding name of 'biblical minimalism,' a revisionist history championed by Northern European professors sometimes called the Copenhagen School. To bolster Arab claims to the region, they sought to disprove the existence of Iron Age Israel, but the facts were in their way. So, they alleged that some of the most famous biblical artifacts may have been 'planted' by Israeli archaeologists (a libel echoing the 'Zionist laundering' allegations above), and for other texts they made up later dates to fit their political narrative. Biblical archaeologist William G. Dever soundly dismantled their claims, simply by reminding us of existing data.[22]

Still, academic dishonesty marched on, infamously repackaged by Nadia Abu El-Haj. In her book *Facts on the Ground*, she took a novel approach when the data did not support her beliefs. Confronted with all the evidence, she dismissed the very concept of 'facts' in order to deny the legitimacy of any Jewish connection to Israel.[23] Her more recent fixation has been Jewish genetics.[24]

Such scholarly misinformation has enabled a set of closely related and widely debunked conspiracy theories including 'Temple Denialism' which rejects any Jewish connection to Jerusalem,[25] the myth that Ashkenazi Jews are not descended from ancient Israelites but rather the medieval Khazars,[26] and Holocaust denial.[27,28] Often invoked together, the aim is to wipe Jews out of the pages of history, along with the pages of history themselves. To this brand of ideologues, the ancient world is a tidy place where disfavored peoples can have their entire existence rejected because it does not fit the trendy dogma of the day. With hundreds of signatories to this most recent propaganda, the geyser has burst. When scholars, who are trusted to be impartial and objective, shirk their duties in responsibly handling data, it paves the way for the public to accept more easily other hoaxes like the popular but nonsensical anti-Christian slogan 'Jesus was a Palestinian.'[29] Wrong again. Jesus was a Jew.

My colleagues have abdicated their scholarly integrity in order to make a political point. Their agenda is clear. Namely, Jewish indigeneity is inconvenient to them because it renders the frequent labeling of the State of Israel as a 'settler colony' absurd. How can a people colonize their own homeland? Hence, one of their cornerstone myths would be demolished. Rather, it already has been, again and again, but they refuse to accept it. Instead, they continue to push that Jews are not ancestral to Israel, and so have no right to be there. As if, even if this were true, such a reality would condone rape and violent genital mutilation as legitimate strategies of resistance – these are some of the 'events' of October 7 that my colleagues call 'not unprovoked.'[30,31] To anti-Zionists, Israeli Jews are always to blame, always the aggressors, and never the victims. By existing, they were asking for it. Would the signatories be so callous if non-Jewish women and girls were raped and mutilated? Such misogynistic double standards have no place in the academy, or anywhere else.

No wonder the public trust in higher education, and in the humanities in particular, has eroded so deeply. Apparently, academic freedom on the American campus in 2023 entitles faculty and students to their own facts and gives sanctuary to the spread of misinformation.

The statement betrays other double standards in the ethical best practices the signatories should have learned in how to treat persecuted descendant communities. For any other modern stakeholders of cultural heritage, my colleagues would attack even the slightest hint of encroachment by any outsider denying ancestral connections to their homeland, to their right of sovereignty, self-defense, and self-determination, and to their own definitions of what discrimination against them entails. Consider another one of their sentences: 'we reject each and every effort to conflate anti-Zionism with anti-Semitism.' What right do they have to define antisemitism? Do they feel entitled to impose their own terms of discrimination on other oppressed minorities, or just on Jews? So, by gaslighting Jews as stakeholders, who equate antisemitism[32] with anti-Zionist rallying cries for the violent eradication of just a single nation-state, the Jewish one, then we see that it is my colleagues themselves who have become the colonizers.

Despite their desire for things to be black and white, the past is complex. For example, the Romans killed or expelled most of the Jews from Judah following the Second Jewish Revolt in AD 132 (today we would call that 'ethnic cleansing').[33] Perhaps to spite the rebellious Jews, the Romans changed the name of the province from *Judaea* to *Syria Palaestina*.[34]

The new namesake was after the ancient Israelites' extinct enemy, the Philistines (the origin of the word 'Palestine') – themselves Greek-speaking migrants from the Mycenaean Aegean[35] – who landed on the shores of Canaan as one of the so-called Sea Peoples in the 12th century BC. By the 6th century BC, they had completely assimilated with indigenous Canaanite groups or were exiled by the Neo-Babylonians, and no one called themselves a 'Philistine' anymore.[36,37]

Just over 500 years after the Second Jewish Revolt, a Muslim army from the Arabian Peninsula invaded and conquered Jerusalem and the rest of the Levant.[38] Although the colonists likely intermarried with local Greek- and Aramaic-speaking inhabitants, soon any pre-Islamic or pre-Arab identity was discarded.[39] Now, it is fashionable to call only their descendants indigenous.

Other academics in the humanities and social sciences must join me in denouncing such misinformation. If instead they come to agree with these signatories that the badge of indigeneity extends only to groups that occupied a land in later times, and not to its previous inhabitants, and censure as 'unlawful' a people's UN-sanctioned repatriation to their ancestral homeland after forced exile and the loss of over a third of their population to Nazi genocide, then they will have condemned the entire post-colonial project as meaningless. This would be a shame. History often involves multiple groups of people with competing claims to the same land. As scholars of the past, it is our duty to faithfully record all of these interactions, whether we like them or not.

Notes

1 https://docs.google.com/document/d/1n-LMsAwR54Vj469Fk7PakavcTY1cw Wb8ga0rEqsgrkw/edit

2 Willick, J. (2023). We Can't Ignore the Truth that Hamas Uses Human Shields. *The Washington Post*, November 14: https://www.washingtonpost.com/opinions/ 2023/11/14/hamas-human-shields-tactic/

3 Kirby, J. (2023). *Press Briefing by Press Secretary Karine Jean-Pierre and NSC Coordinator for Strategic Communications John Kirby*. December 13, 2023, The White House, Washington, DC: https://www.whitehouse.gov/briefing-room/press-briefings/2023/12/13/press-briefing-by-press-secretary-karine-jean-pierre-and-nsc-coordinator-for-strategic-communications-john-kirby-33/

4 Awad, O. (2023). *On the 75th Annual Commemoration of the Palestinian Nakba, Number of Palestinians Worldwide Doubled about 10 Times*. Palestinian Central Bureau of Statistics: https://www.pcbs.gov.ps/post.aspx?lang=en&ItemID=4506

5 Mazar, E. (2009). *The Palace of King David. Excavations at the Summit of the City of David: Preliminary Report of Seasons 2005-2007*. Jerusalem, Israel and New York, NY: Shoham Academic Research and Publication, specifically pp. 66–71.

6 Biran, A. and Naveh, J.. (1993). An Aramaic Stele Fragment from Tel Dan. *Israel Exploration Journal*, 43(2/3), pp. 81–98.

7 Oppenheim, A.L. (1978). Babylonian and Assyrian Historical Texts. Sennacherib (704–681): (a) The Siege of Jerusalem. In: Pritchard, J.B., ed. *Ancient Near Eastern Texts Relating to the Old Testament*. Princeton, NJ: Princeton University Press, pp. 287–288.

8 Zadok, R. (2015). Israelites and Judaeans in the Neo-Assyrian Documentation (743–602 B.C.E.): An Overview of the Sources and a Socio-Historical Assessment. *Bulletin of the American Schools of Oriental Research* 374, pp. 159–189.

9 Bloch, Y. (2014). Judeans in Sippar and Susa during the First Century of the Baby-lonian Exile: Assimilation and Perseverance under Neo-Babylonian and Achaeme-nid Rule. *Journal of Ancient Near Eastern History* 1(2), pp. 119–172.

10 Cline, E. (2005). *Jerusalem Besieged: From Ancient Canaan to Modern Israel.* Ann Arbor, MI: The University of Michigan Press, specifically pp. 119–131.

11 Rendsburg, G.A. (2019). *How the Bible is Written.* Peabody, MA: Hendrickson Publishers.

12 Collins, J.J. and Lim, T.H., eds. *The Oxford Handbook of the Dead Sea Scroll.* Oxford, UK and New York, NY: Oxford University Press.

13 For genetics, see Rosenberg, N.A. and Weitzman, S.P. (2013). From Genera-tion to Generation: The Genetics of Jewish Populations. *Human Biology* 85(6), pp. 817–823, as well as the other contributions to the journal issue.

14 For example, William F. Albright, Benjamin Mazar, Nelson Glueck, James B. Pritchard, Trude Dothan, Kathleen Kenyon, Joseph Naveh, Frank Moore Cross, Avraham Biran, Nadav Na'aman, Amihai Mazar, Amnon Ben-Tor, Jack M. Sasson, Gary A. Rendsburg, William Schniedewind, Ayelet Gilboa, Yosef Garfinkel, Gabriel Barkay, Jodi Magness, Ann E. Killebrew, Steven Ortiz, Eric H. Cline, Aaron A. Burke, Alice Mandell, and there are more.

15 Gordon, C.H. (1968). Northwest Semitic Texts in Latin and Greek Letters. *Journal of the American Oriental Society*, 88(2), pp. 285–289.

16 Astour, M.C. (1965). *Hellenosemitica: An Ethnic and Cultural Study in West Se-mitic Impact on Mycenaean Greece.* Leiden: E.J. Brill.

17 Bernal, M. (1987). *Black Athena: The Afroasiatic Roots of Classical Civilization, Volume I: The Fabrication of Ancient Greece (1785-1985).* New Brunswick, NJ: Rutgers University Press.

18 Morris, S.P. (1992). *Daidalos and the Origins of Greek Art.* Princeton, NJ: Prince-ton University Press.

19 Burkert, W. (1992). *The Orientalizing Revolution: Near Eastern Influence on Greek Culture in the Early Archaic Age.* Cambridge, MA and London: Harvard University Press.

20 López-Ruiz, C. (2021). *Phoenicians and the Making of the Mediterranean.* Cam-bridge, MA and London: Harvard University Press.

21 Bernal (1987), p. 426.

22 Dever, W.G. (2001). *What Did the Biblical Writers Know & When Did They Know It?* Grand Rapids, MI and Cambridge, UK: William B. Eerdmans Publishing Com-pany, specifically pp. 29–30.

23 Abu El-Haj, N. (2001). *Facts on the Ground: Archaeological Practice and Ter-ritorial Self-Fashioning in Israeli Society.* Chicago, IL and London: University of Chicago Press.

24 Abu El-Haj, N. (2012). *The Genealogical Science: The Search for Jewish Origins and the Politics of Epistemology.* Chicago, IL and London: The University of Chicago Press.

25 Wald, J. (2019). The New Replacement Theory: Anti-Zionism, Antisemitism, and the Denial of History. In: Rosenfeld, A.H., ed. *Anti-Zionism and Antisemitism: The Dynamics of Delegitimization.* Bloomington, IN: Indiana University Press.

26 Behar, D.M., Metspalu, M., Baran, Y., Kopelman, N.M., Yunusbayen, B., Gladstein, A., Tzur, S., Sahakyan, H., Bahmanimehr, A., Yepiskoposyan, L., Tambets, K., Khusnutdinova, E.K., Kushniarevich, A., Balanovsky, O., Balanovsky, E., Kovacevic, L., Marjanovic, D., Mihailov, E., Kouvatsi, A., Triantaphyllidis, C.,

King, R.J., Semino, O., Torroni, A., Hammer, M.F., Metspalu, E., Skorecki, K., Rosset, S., Halperin, E., Villems, R., and Rosenberg, N.A. (2013). No Evidence from Genome-Wide Data of a Khazar Origin for the Ashkenazi Jews. *Human Biology* 85(6), pp. 859–900.

27 Middle East Media Research Institute (MEMRI) (2023). *Palestinian Officials Defend Palestinian Authority President Mahmoud Abbas' Remarks on Holocaust and Jews.* Palestinian Authority, Special Dispatch 10806, September 21: https://www.memri.org/reports/palestinian-officials-defend-palestinian-authority-president-mahmoud-abbas-remarks-holocaust

28 Middle East Media Research Institute (MEMRI) (2023). *Syrian President Bashar Al-Assad: There is No Evidence Six Million Jews were Killed in the Holocaust,* December 18: https://www.memri.org/tv/syria-president-bashar-al-assad-holocaust-false-pretext-jews-nazis-khazar-palestine

29 Cope. J. (2023). Jesus was Not Palestinian, We Need to Dispel that Myth Forever. *The Jerusalem Post*, December 24: https://www.jpost.com/opinion/article-779313

30 Rubin, S. (2023). Israel Investigates an Elusive, Horrific Enemy: Rape as a Weapon of War. *The Washington Post*, November 25: https://www.washingtonpost.com/world/2023/11/25/israel-hamas-rape-sexual-violence/

31 Gettleman, J., Schwartz, A., and Sella, A. (2023). "Screams Without Words": How Hamas Weaponized Sexual Violence on Oct. 7. *The New York Times*, December 28: https://www.nytimes.com/2023/12/28/world/middleeast/oct-7-attacks-hamas-israel-sexual-violence.html

32 The consensus definition of antisemitism among mainstream Jewish organizations is that of the International Holocaust Remembrance Alliance: https://www.holocaustremembrance.com/resources/working-definitions-charters/working-definition-antisemitism

33 Raviv, D. and Ben David, C. (2021). Cassius Dio's Figures for the Demographic Consequences of the Bar Kokhba War: Exaggeration or Reliable Account? *Journal of Roman Archaeology* 34, pp. 585–607.

34 Eck, W. (1999). The Bar Kokhba Revolt: The Roman Point of View. *The Journal of Roman Studies* 89, pp. 76–89, specifically pp. 88–89.

35 Dothan, T. (1982). *The Philistines and their Material Culture.* New Haven, CT and London: Yale University Press and, Jerusalem, Israel: The Israel Exploration Society.

36 Maeir, A.M. (2013). Philistia Transforming: Fresh Evidence from Tell Es-Safi/Gath on the Transformational Trajectory of the Philistine Culture. In: Killebrew, A.E. and Lehmann, G., eds. *The Philistines and Other "Sea Peoples" in Text and Archaeology.* Atlanta, GA: Society of Biblical Literature No. 15, pp. 191–242, specifically pp. 193–194.

37 Salameh, F. (2023). Jews, Muslims, and an "Origin Story" of the Arab-Israeli Conflict. *The Caravan Notebook.* The Hoover Institution: https://www.hoover.org/research/jews-muslims-and-origin-story-arab-israeli-conflict

38 Bahat, D. and Rubenstein, C.T. (1996). The Early Arab Period, (639-1099). *The Illustrated Atlas of Jerusalem.* Jerusalem, Israel: Carta, pp. 80–89.

39 Salameh, F. (2010). *Language, Memory, and Identity in the Middle East: The Case for Lebanon.* Lexington Books, specifically pp. xi–12.

11 From Eighteenth-Century Germany to Contemporary Academia

Combating the Conspiracy Theory of Antisemitism in Scholarship

Rebecca Cypess

During the autumn of 2023, I participated in two panels addressing the subject of antisemitism in music and music studies. The first, in late September, was a discussion organized by the Washington Bach Consort on anti-Judaism in the St. John Passion of Johann Sebastian Bach.[1] The second was a session titled 'Antisemitism, Music, and Music Studies: Views from the Field', convened by the Jewish Studies and Music Study Group of the American Musicological Society at the society's annual meeting in early November. I had intended to use the material from my first set of remarks as the basis of the second. Hamas's attack on Israel on 7 October meant that plan was no longer viable. That attack and the resulting war between Israel and Hamas left me not only consumed by grief, worry, and guilt, but, like so many professors, called to a battle of my own—a battle on my university campus and in academia more widely. Yet there is a through-line that links the anti-Judaism in Bach's music to the antisemitism that we are now witnessing within universities: a willingness to indulge conspiracy theories that suppress the full truth and foreclose informed, reasoned discourse. (I follow Gavin Langmuir in distinguishing between the religiously motivated 'anti-Judaism' of the pre-modern era and modern 'antisemitism', which, from its inception in the nineteenth century, based its prejudice against Jews on the flawed 'sciences' of race and ethnicity, and which has, more recently, assumed political dimensions, as well.[2])

For many years, J. S. Bach was my 'desert island' composer—that is, if stranded on a desert island, the one composer whose works I would have taken with me, whose music I felt I could not live without, was Bach. Since high school, when I first came under the spell of early music and period instruments, I have been transfixed by Bach's music—by its beauty and its profundity. The aria 'Es ist vollbracht' (It is finished) from Bach's St. John Passion is a case in point: a heart-wrenching dialogue between an alto soloist and the speechless accompaniment of a viola da gamba, the aria is a lament that dramatizes the seemingly universal experience of pain.[3] Yet this apparent universality is deceptive: a setting of one of the seven last statements attributed

DOI: 10.4324/9781003497424-11

to Jesus on the cross, 'Es ist vollbracht' is about *Christian* suffering brought about, allegedly, by Jewish malfeasance.

Bach was immersed and participated in a virulently anti-Jewish theology, and this theology is inextricable from his music.[4] In the eighteenth century, Jews were banned from living in Saxony; they were allowed to enter Leipzig, where Bach spent most of his life and career, only during the trade fairs, when their business acumen was needed. Yet anti-Judaism was deeply embedded in the supersessionist theology that dominated early eighteenth-century Leipzig—a theology to which Bach not only subscribed, but contributed, as what Robin Leaver calls a 'musical theologian'.[5] Through his musical settings, Bach enhanced and amplified the anti-Jewish sentiment espoused by early modern Lutheranism. While 'Es ist vollbracht' represents the grief inspired by the crucifixion through the most moving music I know, other portions of the St. John Passion portray the Jews as barbaric murderers who demanded the blood of God and were responsible for his death. For example, Bach depicts the Jews screaming, 'Weg, weg mit dem, kreuzige ihn!' (Away, away with him, crucify him!) with a chaotic ferocity that exemplifies what Ruth HaCohen has called 'the music libel against the Jews'—a millennia-old tradition that views Jews as inherently noisy, sonically disruptive, and ethically incapable of making true music.[6]

I first came face-to-face with Bach's religiously motivated anti-Judaism as an undergraduate student at Cornell University in the late 1990s, when the Music Department mounted a performance of the St. John Passion. In preparation for this event, musicologist Michael Marissen was invited to share his research on anti-Judaism in the piece,[7] and I, a mere 20-year-old, was asked to participate in a panel discussion with him on the subject. It was a rude awakening—a first step in my struggle to come to terms with the ugly side of my desert island composer.

Since that time, Marissen has given lecture after lecture, published essays upon books, in which he lays out the clear evidence for Bach's anti-Judaism.[8] For 25 years, he has been continually dismissed by large segments of the Bach community—scholars, performers, and enthusiasts alike. Bach apologists come in two forms: first are those who suggest that Bach gained exposure to—and espoused—ideas of the early Enlightenment that had begun to circulate in early eighteenth-century Leipzig.[9] This notion flies in the face of the extensive documentary evidence that Marissen has assembled. Second are those scholars who simply deny that the sources say what they say. As Marissen notes, until 1945, German musicologists regularly celebrated Bach's convincing portrayals of the barbarity of the Jews, with the nineteenth-century Bach biographer Carl Hermann Bitter even remarking on Bach's adept settings of the 'wildly roaring torrent of Jewry' and, indeed, of the Jews' 'terrorism'.[10] Since 1945, such scholarly celebrations of Bach's anti-Judaism have ceased; many Bach scholars have claimed, simply, that Bach's librettos were not referring to Jews at all, but only to 'priests', or to some other, generalized foil for eighteenth-century Lutherans. Marissen can only lament that 'so many intelligent and decent people … cling to modern views of Bach and his output that are patently contradicted by all available evidence, both reportorial and biographical'.[11]

The gaslighting that Marissen has encountered may be a result of the musical community's investment in Bach's legacy. His work has been canonized—even sacralized and ritualized—to an extent that far exceeds anything that he experienced during his own lifetime. This process of canonization began in the nineteenth century and continues to this day.[12] While the Washington Bach Consort is to be commended for convening a discussion to grapple with Bach's anti-Judaism now, its continued adherence to a triennial cycle of performances of Bach's St. John Passion, St. Matthew Passion, and B-Minor Mass perpetuates this ritualization. As of this writing, the ensemble's website features a statement by the group's founder, J. Reilly Lewis, that confirms this view: 'I've seen people with the most diverse backgrounds come together in one place and be touched by the hand of God through the inspiration—the genius—of Bach, or Brahms or Verdi or Mozart.'[13] This approach is widespread. If scholars, performers, and aficionados of Bach's music view him as a vessel of God, it is easy to understand why they would also seek to protect his reputation. Yet protecting Bach's reputation has meant denying the evidence, which in turn simply serves to perpetuate Bach's legacy of anti-Judaism rather than confronting and challenging it.

For my part, over the past ten years, I have done what I can to divorce Bach's legacy from the anti-Jewish context in which it was born, especially by exploring the reception of his music in the late eighteenth century by Jewish women.[14] That work has given me a point of entry to engagement with my desert island composer. Yet, while the beauty of Bach's sacred vocal music still speaks to me, I have been unable to listen to it since 7 October—not just the St. John Passion, Cantata 46, and other overtly anti-Jewish works, but all of it. I will not argue that listening to this music is wrong, but for me, it is a tainted pleasure that I am unable to allow myself at present. Tractate Gittin (7a) of the Babylonian Talmud suggests that all music should cease as a sign of mourning following the destruction of the ancient Temple in Jerusalem. This prohibition on music has never seemed as relevant to me as it has since 7 October.

While the anti-Judaism in Bach's music and its denial within Bach studies might seem quite distant from Hamas's attacks on Israel and the resulting battles now raging within academia, I view these issues as closely linked. Historian Bernard Lewis showed how the Nazi propaganda machine, which revered Bach and other distinctly German composers, cultivated German-style antisemitism within the Arab world,[15] and the collaboration of Arab leaders with Nazism, as well as their adoption of Nazi propaganda today, are likewise well documented.[16] Joseph S. Spoerl has identified the common thread connecting Nazi and Islamist antisemitism as the conspiratorial thinking that understands 'global Jewry as an enemy conspiring to subjugate and ultimately destroy non-Jews'.[17] While the religious anti-Judaism of Bach's day evolved into the racial and ethnic antisemitism of the nineteenth century and its multi-faceted religious, racial, ethnic, and political manifestations in the modern era, aspects of that anti-Jewish conspiracy theory have remained consistent. The supersessionist belief espoused by early modern Lutheranism that Jews continued to bear guilt for deicide was itself a manifestation of the conspiracy theory that Jews were seeking to destroy civilization.

Journalist Yair Rosenberg lucidly summarized the problem of antisemitism as a conspiracy theory when he testified before the U.S. House Foreign Affairs Committee in June 2023. He explained that antisemitism differs from other forms of bigotry in which groups are despised because they are different: 'too Black, too Brown, too Muslim, too Jewish'. He continues, 'Antisemitism *is* a personal prejudice. But it is also something else: a conspiracy theory about how the world works that blames sinister string-pulling Jews for social and political problems.'[18] The Jewish action organization T'ruah enumerates the common stereotypes that propagate antisemitism: 'Claims that Jews are all-powerful secret puppet masters behind the scenes of world events.' 'Claims that Jews love money, or control the world's financial system or the media.' 'Claims that Jews are untrustworthy and/or disloyal.' 'Claims that Jews are in league with, or are children of, the Devil; that Jews drink blood or kill babies; and that Jews are a corrupting, inhuman force.'[19] Antisemitism's nature as a conspiracy theory explains why it is held by people across the political spectrum and why it is so difficult to identify and eradicate.

Almost as shocking as the brutality of Hamas's 7 October attack has been the speed and ease with which much of the world—including large parts of the academic world—has reverted to these age-old tropes of antisemitism and Jew-hatred. It has now become commonplace not only to justify but to celebrate the litany of Hamas's heinous behaviors, perpetrated primarily against civilians from the youngest babies to the oldest Holocaust survivors. Such sentiments are sometimes overt, as in the so-called 'toolkit' distributed by the national organization Students for Justice in Palestine, which called on its adherents to reframe the 7 October attack as 'morally just and politically necessary'.[20] In other cases, the reversion to Jew-hatred is implicit, as when U.N. Secretary General António Guterres first said that he 'condemned un-equivocally the horrifying and unprecedented 7 October acts of terror', but then, indeed, equivocated by blaming the victims.[21]

Those who engage in such justification and victim blaming are activating the ancient assumption that Jews are disproportionately, unfairly powerful. They imply or state overtly that the Israelis who perished, were tortured, or were abducted on 7 October deserved their fate, or, indeed, that Jews world-wide deserve a similar fate. They claim that all Israelis are white colonialists—never mind that demographics and history contradict that account.[22] They claim that Jews are so bloodthirsty as to intentionally target hospitals—never mind that the overwhelming evidence says otherwise,[23] and never mind that

Hamas places its headquarters of terror in hospitals, schools, and other civilian locations, using their own people as human shields and inviting worldwide condemnation when Israel seeks to defend itself.[24] And, inevitably, the deniers have their day, denying the terrible events of 7 October,[25] even though Hamas operatives themselves took videos of their actions and shared some of them online as a component of their psychological warfare. How can intelligent people accept such denial? It's easy if the underlying conspiracy theory is already there—a conspiracy theory in which Jews are obviously evil, disproportionately powerful, drinkers of blood, destroyers of society.

One would think that scholars—those who pride themselves on their depth of knowledge and their skills in careful research—would help to combat such conspiratorial thinking. Yet, instead of illuminating the path to understanding, universities in the U.S. and Europe have played a leading role in this breathtaking moral failure, even participating—consciously or not—in the motivated reasoning driven by the conspiracy theory of antisemitism. Just as many Bach scholars deny Bach's anti-Judaism, apparently because they feel compelled to defend the reputation of this great composer, many scholars across the humanities and social sciences today have shown a disturbing willingness to ignore or deny facts, bend the truth, or outright lie to serve their political agenda.

A crucial aspect of academic culture that enables scholars today to engage in such falsehood is the abuse of the model of the 'scholar-activist', who elevates political or ideological goals above the search for complexity and understanding.[26] On its surface, scholar-activism sounds good. Its defenders will say that ordinary scholars are locked in an ivory tower, removed from real-world problems, while scholar-activists emerge from that tower to change the world for the better. Scholar-activists generally tie their work to questions of race, class, and identity, positioning themselves as bridges between academia and the underprivileged communities they seek to serve. In recent years, the ideal of the scholar-activist has not only grown in popularity; it has also taken on more extreme forms, with some scholar-activists calling for all academic labor to be exercised as a means to a political end.[27] The certainty of scholar-activists that they know the 'right' outcome of the problem they study means that they are sometimes willing to bend the truth or cherry pick from evidence to support that outcome.

Such extreme manifestations of scholar-activism had damaged the prospects of reasoned discourse on the Israeli-Palestinian conflict long before 7 October 2023. The theory that the entire conflict could be reduced to a problem of 'settler-colonialism' is a case in point. Within many applications of the paradigm of settler-colonialism, one is either the oppressor or the oppressed, the colonizer or the colonized. People are sorted into good and bad with remarkable ease. Yet, to cast Israelis universally as white oppressors is to willfully ignore Jews' indigeneity to Israel, their ethnic heterogeneity, their history of victimhood and migration in the twentieth- and twenty-first centuries, the rejection of peace by generations of Palestinian leaders, and the fact that Israel is a racially, ethnically, and religiously diverse society that includes many Arabs and people of wide-ranging origins and heritages as full citizens.[28] That the simplistic application of the settler-colonialist paradigm to the Israeli-Palestinian conflict has repeatedly passed the peer-review process is a sign of the problematic nature of that process. When such unnuanced application of theory makes its way into the peer-reviewed literature, it contributes to the erosion of public trust in the humanities and social sciences.

Scholar-activism has apparently also contributed to the ongoing Boycott, Divestment, and Sanctions (BDS) movement against Israel. By seeking to remove Israeli scholars and institutions from the international community of learning, the BDS movement suppresses and ignores the perspective of an entire population. While proponents of BDS claim to take the moral high ground by pressing for political change, they instead foreclose discussion by refusing to take in the complete picture. A case in point is the National Women's Studies Association, which adopted BDS with the assent of nearly 90% of its members in 2015.[29] If NWSA had not been so quick to excise Israeli perspectives, perhaps one of the two statements that the group has issued since 7 October 2023, might have acknowledged Hamas's brutal rape and mutilation of Israeli women that day.[30] Instead, like many human rights groups, women's advocacy groups, and scholarly societies worldwide, NWSA has remained silent on this issue.[31] The inconvenient testimony and forensic evidence concerning Hamas's heinous acts do not align with the narrative of NWSA's self-styled 'activists'.[32] Those perspectives, along with the documented, routine mistreatment of women in areas controlled by Hamas and the Palestinian Authority, are thus easily swept aside.[33]

Insidiously, the model of scholar-activism has come to inform student-facing structures within academia. While it is perhaps understandable that university offices of Diversity, Equity, and Inclusion in the U.S. have focused primarily on race and ethnicity because of that country's history of racism, they have been virtually silent about the current wave of antisemitism sweeping across universities today. In some cases, DEI offices have been resistant even to educating their communities about antisemitism, because they are afraid of appearing to 'take a side'—as if the issue were whether universities should be in favor of antisemitism or not. In assuming these stances, such offices are conveying their tacit adoption of antisemitic tropes like 'all Jews are unfairly powerful', which leads them to assume that Jews neither need nor deserve protection.

Given the ease with which universities have reverted to antisemitism, is it any wonder that Jews in academia feel such a profound sense of betrayal? I have devoted my adult life to higher education, and I feel that I have watched it collapse overnight. My sense of loss was driven home when I read a 'Letter of Deep Concern from University Heads in Israel' written in early November. In addition to stating what should be an obvious point—'Hamas shares no values with any Western academic institution'—these university leaders felt compelled to defend Jews in academia outside Israel: 'We expect that Israeli and Jewish students and faculty on university and college campuses will be accorded the same respect and protections as any other minority'.[34] As grateful as I am for the support of Israel's academic leadership, I am deeply ashamed of the fundamental failure of academia that precipitated such a message.

Surely the role of the university must be to pursue and share truth. This requires robust, vigorous debate—not facile slogans, petitions that marked by oversimplification, or, worst of all, activism that masquerades as scholarship while refusing to acknowledge complicating facts. When we hear our students and colleagues revert to the easy answers undergirded by the conspiracy theory of antisemitism, it is incumbent upon us to speak out. Indeed, combating such thinking has become a full-time job for many of us in academia today.

I'll close by citing the words of Paul Frosh, Professor of Communication and Journalism at the Hebrew University of Jerusalem, who addressed an open letter by his colleagues in the UK that ignored the Israeli lives lost on 7 October: 'Your universalism is a universalism of fools: a universalism in which Jews, even dead ones, don't really count. Something has snapped: an uncrossable line has been drawn between us'.[35] Or, to borrow the words of Bach's St. John Passion, 'es ist vollbracht'—it is finished.

Notes

1 Cypess, R. et al. (2023a) 'Bach and Antisemitism'. Panel discussion organized by the Washington Bach Consort. Bethesda, Maryland, USA. 28 September. Available at: https://www.youtube.com/watch?v=3jVI_sNTyiY (Accessed: 26 November 2023).
2 See Langmuir, G. I. (1990) *Toward a Definition of Antisemitism*. Berkeley: University of California Press.
3 Harnoncourt, N., Conductor, Concentus Musicus Wien, and Tölzer Knabenchor. P. Iconomou, Alto Soloist. C. Coin, Viola da Gamba. (1985) 'Alto Aria: "Es ist vollbracht"', from Johann Sebastian Bach, St. John Passion, BWV 245. Deutsche Grammophon B000L21DO4 [Online]. Available at: https://www.youtube.com/watch?v=AOoe8K1yj50&t=68s (Accessed: 2 December 2023).
4 Fischer, L. (2021) 'The Legacy of Anti-Judaism in Bach's Sacred Cantatas', in Aue-Ben David, I. et al. (ed.) *Jews and Protestants: From the Reformation to the Present*. Berlin and Boston: De Gruyter, pp. 71–88.
5 Leaver, R. (2000) 'Johann Sebastian Bach: Theological Musician and Musical Theologian', *Bach: Journal of the Riemenschneider Bach Institute* 31(1), pp. 17–33.
6 Jacobs, R., Conductor, and Akademie für Alte Musik Berlin. (2016) 'Die Jüden aber schrieen und sprachen', from Johann Sebastian Bach, St. John Passion, BWV 245. Harmonia Mundi HMC80223637 [Online]. Available at: https://www.youtube.com/watch?v=bFIRjaNC7GI (Accessed: 2 December 2023); HaCohen, R. (2013) *The Music Libel against the Jews*. New Haven: Yale University Press.
7 Marissen, M. (1998) *Lutheranism, Anti-Judaism, and Bach's St. John Passion*. New York: Oxford University Press.
8 Marissen, M. (2016) *Bach and God*. New York: Oxford University Press; Marissen, M. (2022) *Bach against Modernity*. New York: Oxford University Press.

9 For example, Erikson, R. (2014) 'The Early Enlightenment, Jews, and Bach: Further Considerations', *Understanding Bach* 9, pp. 93–100.

10 Marissen, M. (2022) *Bach against Modernity*. New York: Oxford University Press, p. 143n12.

11 Ibid., p. 24.

12 On the nineteenth-century process of Bach canonization, see Applegate, C. (2005) *Bach in Berlin: Nation and Culture in Mendelssohn's Revival of the 'St. Matthew Passion'*. Ithaca: Cornell University Press.

13 Washington Bach Consort. (no date) 'Mission' [Online]. Available at: https://bachconsort.org/founders-vision/ (Accessed: 2 December 2023).

14 For example, Cypess, R. (2022) *Women and Musical Salons in the Enlightenment*. Chicago: University of Chicago Press, pp. 200–232.

15 For example, Lewis, B. (2006) 'The New Anti-Semitism', *American Scholar* [Online]. Winter. Available at: https://theamericanscholar.org//the-new-anti-semitism/ (Accessed: 3 December 2023).

16 See Herf, J. (2009) *Nazi Propaganda for the Arab World*. New Haven: Yale University Press; Küntzel, M. (2023) *Nazis, Islamic Antisemitism and the Middle East: The 1948 Arab War against Israel and the Aftershocks of World War II. Studies in Contemporary Antisemitism*. London: Routledge; and Rubin, B. and Schwanitz, W. (2014) *Nazis, Islamists, and the Making of the Modern Middle East*. New Haven: Yale University Press.

17 Spoerl, J. S. (2020) 'Parallels between Nazi and Islamist Anti-Semitism', *Jewish Political Studies Review* 31(1–2) [Online]. Available at: https://jcpa.org/article/parallels-between-nazi-and-islamist-anti-semitism/ (Accessed: 3 December 2023).

18 Rosenberg, Y. (2023) 'Testimony of Yair Rosenberg, Staff Writer, *The Atlantic*, House Foreign Affairs Committee, "Responding to Anti-Semitism and Anti-Israel Bias"' June 23 [Online]. Available at: https://docs.house.gov/meetings/FA/FA06/20230622/116138/HHRG-118-FA06-Wstate-RosenbergY-20230622.pdf, p. 2. (Accessed: 5 November 2023).

19 T'ruah. (2022) 'A Very Brief Guide to Antisemitism' [Online]. Available at: https://truah.org/antisemitism/ (Accessed: 26 November 2023). See also Ward, E. and Black, M. (2022) 'Antisemitism' in [s.n.] *Moving Toward Antibigotry: Collected Essays from the Center for Antiracist Research's Antibigotry Convening* [Online]. Available at: https://www.bu.edu/antiracism-center/files/2022/06/Moving-Towards-Antibigotry.pdf (Accessed: 26 November 2023).

20 Students for Justice in Palestine (National Organization). (2023) 'Day of Resistance Toolkit' [Online]. Available at: https://dw-wp-production.imgix.net/2023/10/DAY-OF-RESISTANCE-TOOLKIT.pdf (Accessed: 26 November 2023).

21 Novick, T. (2023) 'No Contextualization without Explanation', *Times of Israel*. 29 October [Online]. Available at: https://blogs.timesofisrael.com/no-contextualization-without-explanation/ (Accessed: 26 November 2023).

22 Central Intelligence Agency. (2023) *The World Factbook: Israel* [Online]. Available at: https://www.cia.gov/the-world-factbook/countries/israel/#:~:text=Jewish%2073.5%25%2C%20Muslim%2018.1%25,4.9%25%20(2022%20est.) (Accessed: 26 November 2023).

23 Xiong, Y. (2023) 'Revisiting a Key Video Used to Assess the Gaza Hospital Blast', *CNN.com*. 2 November [Online]. Available at: https://www.cnn.com/2023/11/02/middleeast/al-jazeera-video-gaza-hospital-blast-intl/index.html (Accessed: 26 November 2023).

24 Reuters and ILH Staff. (2023) 'WATCH: Hamas' Headquarters Inside a Gaza Hospital', *Israel Hayom*. 27 October [Online]. Available at: https://www.israelhayom.com/2023/10/27/watch-hamas-headquarters-inside-a-gaza-hospital/ (Accessed: 26 November 2023); Jaffe-Hoffman, M. (2023) 'Watch: IDF Shares Proof of Hamas

Terror Base Built under Main Gaza Hospital', *Jerusalem Post* [Online]. 27 October. Available at: https://www.jpost.com/middle-east/article-770484 (Accessed: 12 November 2023).

25 Freedman, E. (2023) 'Fearing Denial and Disinformation, Israel Shows Journalists Raw Footage of Hamas Attacks', *Jewish Telegraphic Agency* [Online]. 23 October. Available at: https://www.jta.org/2023/10/23/israel/fearing-denial-and-disinformation-israel-shows-journalists-raw-footage-of-hamas-attacks (Accessed: 5 November 2023).

26 Cypess, R. (2023b) 'The Abuse of Scholar-Activism', *Inside Higher Ed* [Online]. 13 December. Available at: https://www.insidehighered.com/opinion/views/2023/12/13/scholar-activism-contributes-antisemitism (Accessed: 24 December 2023).

27 Young, A.M., Battaglia, A., and Cloud, D.L. (2010) '(UN)Disciplining the Scholar Activist: Policing the Boundaries of Political Engagement', *Quarterly Journal of Speech* 96(4), November, pp. 427–435.

28 Central Intelligence Agency. (2023) *The World Factbook: Israel* [Online]. Available at: https://www.cia.gov/the-world-factbook/countries/israel/#:~:text=Jewish%2073.5%25%2C%20Muslim%2018.1%25,4.9%25%20(2022%20est.) (Accessed: 26 November 2023).

29 Redden, E. (2015) 'Another Association Backs Israel Boycott', *Inside Higher Education* [Online]. Available at: https://www.insidehighered.com/news/2015/12/01/national-womens-studies-association-joins-israel-boycott-movement (Accessed: 3 December 2023).

30 National Women's Studies Association. (2023a) 'Archive of NWSA Presidential Statements & Membership Newsletters' [Online]. Available at: https://www.nwsa.org/page/statements (Accessed: 3 December 2023).

31 Botbol, A. (2023a) 'Global Women's Rights Groups Silent as Israeli Women Testify About Rapes by Hamas', *Times of Israel*. 23 November [Online]. Available at: https://www.timesofisrael.com/global-womens-rights-groups-silent-as-israeli-women-testify-about-rapes-by-hamas/ (Accessed: 3 December 2023).

32 National Women's Studies Association. (2023b) 'Membership' [Online]. Available at: https://www.nwsa.org/page/Membership (Accessed: 3 December 2023).

33 U.S. Department of State, Bureau of Democracy, Human Rights, and Labor. No date. 'Custom Report Excerpts: Israel, West Bank. Section 6. Discrimination, Societal Abuses, and Trafficking in Persons' [Online]. Available at: https://www.state.gov/report/custom/6a63b4154c/ (Accessed: 3 December 2023).

34 Zaban, A. et al. (2023) 'Letter of Deep Concern from University Heads in Israel to Colleagues around the World'. 1 November [Online] https://www.technion.ac.il/en/2023/11/55591/?fbclid=IwAR2M70YXQcroHbhRotCYSwyJ2TYN2BYkDVXZ3K-o6iV-mYreSvl-xKJL9mc_aem_AYYP0gttoT0izUaRsMMF-WgnK6E8f5mXVkzUqeL10jCqs91Vm5siKInzEiX9fIuQUzY&mibextid=Zxz2cZ (Accessed: 5 November 2023).

35 Frosh, P. (2023) 'Open Letter to the Signatories of "Letter by media & communications scholars on British news media coverage of the war in Gaza"'. 20 October. *Facebook.com* [Online] https://www.facebook.com/902990083/posts/open-letter-to-the-signatories-of-letter-by-media-communications-scholars-on-bri/10168024034100084/ (Accessed: 5 November 2023).

Index

Printed and bound by CPI Group (UK) Ltd, Croydon, CR0 4YY

08/10/2024

01042240-0004